Platonism and the

Essays by
John M Dillon
Brendan O'Byrne
Tim Addey

The Prometheus Trust
in association with

The Dublin Centre
for the Study of the Platonic Tradition

The Prometheus Trust
28 Petticoat Lane
Dilton Marsh
Westbury
Wiltshire, BA13 4DG

A registered charity no. 299628

Platonism and the World Crisis
Second edition

John M Dillon
Brendan O'Byrne
Tim Addey

ISBN 978 1 898910 55 8

Published 2010, Westbury

British Library Cataloguing-in-Publication Data.
A catalogue record for this book is available from the British Library.

Printed in the UK by Remous Ltd, Sherborne.

Contents

Towards a Philosophic Democracy

Tim Addey

It falls to me to introduce this second edition of *Platonism and the World Crisis*: a task which is both a delight and something of a responsibility. The delight arises from the clarity of the essays from both John Dillon and Brendan O'Byrne, which together with their perspective that enables the wider picture to be seen, brings to our attention the fundamental choice that lies before humankind at the beginning of the twenty-first century – the choice between the headlong pursuit of wealth measured in material terms, or the cultivation of *arete* (or virtue) together with the balance indicated by Socrates at the conclusion of the *Phaedrus* in which he prays that "whatever I possess externally may be friendly to my inward attainment." The responsibility stems from the stark contrast between the likely outcomes of the two paths that, broadly speaking, lie onwards from that fundamental choice: on one side a world in which humanity loses sight of its own nature with all the dreadful consequences to ourselves, to our emerging world society, and to our planet. On the other side, a virtuous circle in which an intelligent approach to our activities concerned with our environment, our society and our inner life will enable the recovery of that faculty which Socrates said[1] was worth "ten thousand eyes" and which allows us to see the truth of our selves, and to understand our proper relationships with each other as well as with the natural world. From such a vision would arise yet more harmonious inner and outer activities, for as the Platonic tradition tells us, *knowledge is virtue*.

The two essays, *The Urgency of Platonism* and *Platonism and the World Crisis*, complement each other well: in the first Brendan O'Byrne traces the development of our current worldview at a theoretical

[1] *Republic* 527e.

level, while in the second John Dillon addresses some of the most obvious problems which such a worldview brings about – and this he does in a most practical fashion. Two of the three problems which are tackled – those of our environment and our *polis* – are offered solutions which could be enacted should we find the political will so to do; the third – that of religious conflict – while being less susceptible to purely political direction, is nevertheless approached in the same spirit, with some clear guidance regarding the specific ways in which present religious attitudes need to be changed.

What both essays show, each in their own way, is that the highlighted problems of modern humankind are primarily *failures of its philosophy*, and only secondarily those of behaviour: so while it is tempting to look for purely practical solutions to our world problems, this option is not open to us – if we try so to do, we will merely exchange one set of difficulties for other, equally painful ones. Real solutions can only arise from a fundamental revision of philosophy.

The question which arises from the juxtaposition of the two essays is whether or not humankind can enact the solutions (or something like them) offered in John Dillon's essay? Can we reverse many hundreds of years of accumulating materialism in the short time we have before we are overwhelmed by the ill effects of it? The thought, they say, is father to the deed: and because our thoughts are more or less shaped by our worldview, we might justly claim that that worldview is grandfather to the deed. It is possible, of course, that this book will become a world best-seller, that the millions who read it will immediately recognise the sound good sense of the solutions it offers, and resolve to enact them – in which case we can look forward to a happier future than seems likely under our present circumstances. But for this to happen there will have to be a fundamental shift in our collective thought-world: how is this to happen?

One of the great myths of ancient Greece concerned that of two brothers, Prometheus and Epimetheus: Epimetheus was given the task of distributing natural gifts to all the creatures of the world – speed, strength, fur, sharp claws, horns, stings, and so on – but he did not plan ahead (his name means 'after thought') and so when he came to bestow a gift on the last animal – man – he had nothing left and the poor creature was left naked and defenceless. It was then that Prometheus intervened in order to provide for humankind – he stole the fire of heaven and gave it to them in place of the more physical attributes distributed by his brother. Prometheus also taught the human race how to make sacrifices to the Gods using this new gift of divine fire.

The story, amongst many other truths, establishes two ways in which creatures can live: one is through that kind of knowledge which arises *after* experience, a more external knowledge which is inevitably mixed with pleasure and pain. This knowledge is slow to inform thinking creatures about the right ways to deal with new situations, because it relies upon the reception of pleasure and pain after a particular approach to it has been tried. The alternative is the Promethean way, which uses forethought to consider things *before* the experience of particular activities – the name Prometheus means 'fore thought.' What we can be fairly certain about is that Westernised global society will change itself as a result of the tripartite crisis outlined in Dillon's essay – but will it change through Promethean forethought, or will the change be Epimethean, following the pain which will arise if we do not address our problems now? From every point of view, it is better that the Promethean way is taken, and I am convinced that men and women everywhere should be working towards ensuring that we do so.

4

Now Pausanias[2] tells us that in Plato's Academy there was an altar to Prometheus from which races were run through the city of Athens – each runner carried a torch (presumably lit from the altar) which upon pain of disqualification could not be allowed to go out. It seems entirely appropriate that the most distinguished centre of philosophy in the West honoured Prometheus in this way: true philosophy – that is to say philosophy as the love of wisdom – is the means *par excellence* whereby we develop our Promethean powers. Philosophy, as understood by the Platonic tradition, requires us to explore ideas firstly as separated from their material manifestation, and then secondly as informing material: it is the consideration of ideas as *prior* to their manifestation that allows real Promethean foresight. This is in contradistinction to the Epimethean mode of thought which is unable to perceive ideas except in their material instantiation. In the *Republic*,[3] Socrates has this to say about the idea of the good, as an object of human endeavour:

> "This I rather think, since you have often heard at least, that the idea of the good is the greatest discipline: which idea when justice and the other virtues employ, they become useful and advantageous. You now almost know that this is what I mean to say, and besides this, that we do not sufficiently know that idea, and that without this knowledge, though we understood every thing else in the highest degree, you know that it is of no advantage to us: in the same manner as it would avail us nothing though we possessed any thing whatever without the possession of the good: or do you think there is any greater profit in possessing all things without the possession of the good, than in

[2] Pausanias, *Guide to Greece*, I, 30, 2.
[3] *Republic* 505a – the translation is, in common with other extracts throughout, by Thomas Taylor.

knowing all things without the knowledge of the good, knowing nothing at all that is beautiful and good?"

But, says Socrates, most people pursue the good only when it becomes apparent in the shifting world of material manifestation, and consequently mistake pleasure for the good, and so, he continues to Adimantus, [4]

"This then is that which every soul pursues, and for the sake of this it does every thing, prophesying that it is something, but being dubious, and unable to comprehend sufficiently what it is, and to possess the same stable belief respecting it as of other things; and thus are they unsuccessful also in other things, if there be in them any profit. About a thing now of such a kind, and of such mighty consequence, shall we say that even these our best men in the city, and to whom we commit the management of everything, shall be thus in the dark? As little at least as possible, said he. I think then, said I, that whilst it is unknown in what manner the just and beautiful are good, they are not of any great value to a guardian to possess, if it be likely he shall know these, whilst he is ignorant of this; but I prophesy that no one will arrive at the knowledge of these before he sufficiently knows what the good is."

Of course the attempt to see ideas in themselves, separate from material existence, will not be made unless we believe firstly that such ideas have an intrinsic reality independent of the reasoning mind, and secondly that we have the power to perceive them. Both beliefs, so basic to the Platonic tradition, have been seriously questioned in modern times: these challenges are the natural bedfellows of the movement which has sought to abandon *arete*

[4] *Republic* 505e–506a.

6

(excellence or virtue[5]) as the goal of humans, instead promoting material contentment above all other ideals. *Arete,* as the perfect manifestation of the essential nature of anything is an invalid concept if things do not have intrinsic qualities, and if the human rational self is seen as a chance creature arising from the accidents of matter, any virtue we may affirm of ourselves must be seen as yet another convenient construct of the mind - a mere convention, rather than something real.

From the first doubt – that ideas have no intrinsic and independent reality - arises the whole modern theory of relativism. It is a self-negating position, for to deny the reality of ideas is only possible if the denier uses the stability of ideas in order to form his or her thoughts, and re-uses them in their expression in intelligible language. A thorough examination of the falsity of this position (known as anti-realism), is to be found in a forthcoming book, *Metaphysics and Mysticism in Modern Physic: a Revival of Platonic Realism* by John H Spencer,[6] and I leave it to the interested reader to consider the powerful arguments he puts forward against anti-realism. It is the second doubt – that even if absolute and eternal ideas have a transcendent reality, the human mind is incapable of knowing them – which most directly brings about the general problems which Dillon's essay encapsulates as destruction of the environment, religious intolerance and legitimation of authority: it is this doubt and its effects that I would like to comment on.

---

[5] Readers should note that there has been a subtle change of meaning of *virtue* in the Christian era, largely due to the doctrine of original sin: for the Greeks *arete* denotes an excellence arising from the essential nature of a human soul – which itself is not intrinsically sinful, but rather something good and similar to divinity. It is for this reason that Plotinus says in his treatise *On the Virtues* (En. I, ii, 6) that "the endeavour is not to be without sin, but to be a god." Virtue then, in this sense, is not something externally added to the soul, but is grown from its very essence.
[6] Parmenides Publishing, likely to be published in 2010 or 2011.

Western man has placed himself in a curious position in which he simultaneously over- and under-estimates himself. On the one hand he sees himself as master of nature, free to take what he will from the natural world; on the other he disregards the powers which he possesses as a rational soul – powers which if unfolded would lead to a life both "orderly and divine", as Plato puts it.[7] As long as our culture subscribes to this strange view of the nature of the human self, our attempts to establish proper relations with the divine, the manifested cosmos, and with each other will be characterized almost entirely by prohibitions and denials as we try to rein in desires which lead to excesses. Certainly, if one looks to the ecology movement, the message which comes across most clearly is that we should consume less of a whole range of resources. Such an approach is almost certain to fail: every creature has a natural impulse towards happiness, and if human happiness is seen in terms of material consumption that impulse will drive us towards such an end, unhappy as it will ultimately prove to be.

What is required is a radical change in the way we see ourselves and our true goals: we are rational creatures able to contemplate eternal ideas – ideas which are not merely human concepts, but actually living, beautiful, intelligent beings. It is this contemplation which the Platonic tradition holds as the true seat of happiness, the rewards of which far outweigh those of mere material consumption: as Diotima says, concerning the perception of eternal beauty,[8] "what effect, think you, would the sight of beauty itself have upon a man, were he to see it pure and genuine, not corrupted and stained all over with the mixture of flesh, and colours, and much more of like perishing and fading trash; but were able to view that divine essence, the beautiful itself, in its own simplicity of form? Think you that the life of such a

---

[7] *Republic* 500c.
[8] *Symposium* 211c.

man would be contemptible or mean; of the man who always directed his eye toward the right object, who looked always at real beauty, and was conversant with it continually?" She goes on to explain that there is an essential relationship between the cultivation of virtue and the perception of real being (or, in other words, ideas in the Platonic sense of the word), and that by pursuing this path the lover of true Beauty would "become a favourite of the Gods, and would be, if any man ever be, himself one of the immortals."

Philosophy, at least as understood in the Platonic tradition, is the way in which rational creatures unfold their inner qualities – gradually recalling the eternal ideas which the soul saw before it descended into materiality, and at the same time living a life good, wise and beautiful. The way rests upon the truth of the affirmation that *knowledge is virtue* and the self – the soul – is moved by its embrace of real ideas. So that, for example, to know justice truly will be to be just, to know beauty truly will be to be beautiful, to know wisdom truly is to be wise; and to be these things will naturally lead us to act justly, beautifully and wisely. It is this movement and this movement alone which can properly be described as human progress: all other more outward appearances of progress are illusory – the ebb and flow of the ceaseless tide of material existence.

If our society pursues this one form of progress which for human beings is genuinely worthy of the name, we must promulgate *philosophical* education, for as the Guest in the *Laws* says:[9]

> "For now, when we blame or praise the education of particular persons, we say that such a one is endued with discipline, but another is undisciplined, although he may possess the greatest skill in cooking, or navigation, and other things of this kind. For we do not, as it appears, consider these to be discipline, but that

[9] *Laws* 643d-644a.

which causes a citizen from his childhood to desire and love virtue, and through which acquiring perfection, *he may know how to govern and be governed with justice*. This is what our discourse defines to be education; from which it appears, that this alone ought to be called discipline, according to our sentiments; but that the education which tends to the acquisition of wealth, or bodily strength, or any other particular wisdom, without intellect and justice, is mechanical and illiberal, and does not in any respect deserve to be called discipline. We shall not, however, contend about a word. But let what we have just now assented to remain, that those who are properly disciplined become nearly all of them good."

Since it adheres to the beautiful ideas which produce all that is worthwhile in the universe, philosophic[10] education is indeed that which develops a love of virtue, and which leads us to the point at which we may both govern and be governed. Thus we return to the practicalities of instituting the kind of political approach which is discussed in *Platonism and the World Crisis*: how can we encourage governments around the world to adopt the measures which are needed if we are to right our relations to the world, to each other, and to divinity?

Plato famously said that there would be no end to human ills unless philosophers became rulers, or rulers became philosophers.[11] Given that most governments around the world are either genuinely democratic or at least pay lip service to the democratic ideal, it would seem that the way forward is to reset the methods and goals of education to reflect Plato's priorities – the cultivation of virtue and the contemplation of ideas, rather than that which serves merely to

---

[10] Using the term *philosophic* in the sense in which it was understood in the Platonic tradition, rather than its debased meaning of our commercial age.

[11] Cf. *Republic* 473d and *Epistle VII* 326b.

acquire wealth or produce mundane skills. One of the encouraging advances around the world over the past century or so has been the introduction of universal education in one country after another: but now humankind must set itself the task of introducing good philosophy into this universal education – to re-enact the task of Prometheus, and bring the divine fire of wisdom to our otherwise vulnerable race. In other words, to ensure that the democratic decisions that lie before us in our crisis are made by men and women who are aware of the great truths of philosophy.

The world's problems are as much those of wealth as they are of poverty: certainly, the first of Dillon's crisis points (that of the environment) is largely the fault of the so-called developed nations, rather than those of the developing ones. A philosophic education will change our perspective so that, for example, we will consider with Plato,[12] "that poverty consists not in the diminution of property, but in an insatiable desire of acquiring more."

The second crisis point (that of religious intolerance) is also best met by a philosophic education, because it is philosophy which enables us to see the universal that lies behind the many and diverse particularities of life, and the "thing itself" behind the differing names given to it. Philosophy allows us a wider view of ourselves, our fellow humans, and differing religious views – an all-important requisite as we enter an age in which global communications bring various groups into ever-closer contact with each other. As Dillon writes, "we must learn to allegorize our beliefs" – and philosophy is the key to allegory.

The third crisis point (the legitimation of authority) can really only be dealt with by the realist position of Platonic philosophy – or something very like it – because if the view is held that there is no

---

[12] *Laws* 736e.

reality to ideas, then laws (which enshrine ideas as active principles within society) are in turn held to be merely arbitrary dictates of those who chance to be the most powerful. Conversely, if we consider law and political authority to be the reflection of intelligent ideas and the order of the universe, fashioned perhaps somewhat less than perfectly but with the best abilities of law-makers, we will see why Plato has this to say:[13]

> "It is necessary, therefore, that we should always follow the most beautiful guidance of law. For, since the energy of reasoning is beautiful and gentle, but not violent, servants have need of its guidance, that the golden race [i.e. our intellect] in us may vanquish the genera of a different kind [the irrational]. And thus the fable [of the men of the golden age], *since we are beings of a wonderful nature*, will be preservative of virtue . . ."

Good laws arise when law-makers can see clearly the principles that govern and order communities, and when they understand the nature of the individuals that make up their communities: at the end of the last book of the *Republic*, Socrates breaks off from his description of the myth of Er to say that above all things, the discipline which leads to the wisdom which can discern a good life from the bad is necessary. He outlines what this discipline must consider and concludes by saying that such an educated person must,[14] "be able from all these things to compute, and, having an eye to the nature of the soul, to comprehend both the worse and the better life, pronouncing that to be the worse which shall lead the soul to become more unjust, and that to be the better life which shall lead it to become more just, and to dismiss every other consideration."

[13] *Laws* 645a
[14] *Republic* 618e.

It normally takes many years – generations, in fact – to have new concepts and perspectives move from the small circle of leading thinkers who give birth to them, outwards and downwards until they find a place in the ordinary thought-life of the general population. The philosophical steps outlined by O'Byrne which have brought us to our present world crisis – the promotion of *pleonexia,* the triumph of technology and private liberty, and the abandonment of virtue – have just such a history. If good philosophy (by which I mean the Platonic kind) is to be re-established in order to allow us to address intelligently the very severe problems we now face, we cannot afford to think in terms of generations: as the title chosen by O'Byrne for his essay indicates, time presses upon us and at best we may have a decade or two to change our culture's thinking and behaviour. Fortunately we are not advocating new ideas, or a new worldview: as *The Urgency of Platonism* suggests, the arguments required to confront the errors of recent centuries have been set out in the writings of the Platonic tradition. Furthermore, a side effect of the technological revolution we are living through has changed the ways in which ideas spread: there are still hierarchies which direct the communication of leading thought, but the influence of networks is now challenging them.

The philosophic education of the world's population in order to produce philosophic democracies is a huge task, but not an impossible one. It requires efforts to be made within and without academia, inside and outside formal government, in mass communications and in ordinary conversations. Our culture has, by and large, led a Epimethian life – his spouse, Pandora, has come with her box of experiences and the last century has produced some quite horrific ones to add to the old: but Hope was said to be found when all the box's horrors had flown into the world, and hope we must.

Platonism and the World Crisis

John M Dillon

Preface

I am conscious of employing here a somewhat portentous title for what I am about to say, a title which may promise rather more than is actually going to be delivered; but it is in fact my deeply-held conviction that Plato, and the tradition deriving from him, has a number of important things to say to the modern world, to which the modern world would do well to listen. Of course, Plato had no conception of the nature or complexity of the issues with which modern civilisation is currently faced, but nonetheless, it seems to me, there are many useful insights which we may derive both from his own works – in particular his last great work, The Laws – and from those of certain of his followers, in particular Plotinus.

The topics on which I would like to focus my attention on this occasion are just three, but they seem to me to be such as, between them, to represent the great bulk of what is wrong with modern western society, and what is inexorably putting intelligent life on this planet under mortal threat. They are the following:

(1) The problem of the destruction of the environment and of waste disposal.

(2) The problem of religious conflict and mutual intolerance.

(3) The problem of the legitimation of authority and the limits of personal freedom.

On each of these questions it will be found, I think, that Plato has things of importance to say. I will address them in turn.

Prefatory Note to the Second Edition

This essay, or discourse, was composed and delivered originally back in 2006, when the material state of Western civilisation was significantly different to what has since now become. Then we were still on a 'high', fuelled by unlimited oil and dubious financial instruments, quite oblivious to the fact that we were about to suffer a fall of the dimensions of which I must confess I had little inkling, and we were not much inclined to listen to admonitions such as those contained herein. However, all that has changed, and what has happened in these last few years may in fact embody some positive aspects, if we are prepared now at last to sober up somewhat. In my own country of Ireland (to which these remarks were originally directed, as will become obvious) as in the rest of Europe (and even, to some extent, in the US and China), one can now observe a far greater concern for sustainability, recycling of waste, and the development of renewable energy sources. This may yet contribute to our salvation - though much more work needs to be done to realise the plans so far put forward - and the relative failure of the Copenhagen summit is hardly encouraging in this regard. It is at least, however, possible to envisage that, by 2020 or so, Europe might be well on the way to energy self-sufficiency, and large-scale recycling of waste, as well as to overall population balance.

This, however, only addresses the first of my three areas of concern. On the question of religious tolerance, particularly as between Christianity and Islam, very little progress is discernable, but it is possible that the current embarrassment caused to the Catholic Church in the wake of extensive revelations of child abuse and accompanying cover-ups may bring that organisation at least to a more modest frame of mind as regards their possession of an absolute truth which must be imposed on everybody. There has been no corresponding weakening of certainties, so far as I can observe, on the side of Islam, but I believe that there would be reciprocity if overtures were made in the proper spirit. And of course the awful torment of the Palestinian people must be alleviated, as so much of this trouble is traceable to that. There seems some prospect that President Obama is less inclined to act as the poodle-dog of Israel than were his predecessors, but he will have a serious struggle to assert himself in that quarter.

As regards my third issue, respect for and legitimation of authority, the problem is the same. Our leaders have not been covering themselves with glory in the intervening years, and we are no more inclined to embark on programmes of 'national service' for the young. Western democracies have really never worked out any type of 'coming-of-age' or 'rite-of-passage' processes for young people about to become adults, and the pressures on such young people seem to increase with every decade.

So there it is. This pamphlet was originally intended, as I say, for a local audience in Ireland, but copies of it have spread, rather selectively, around the world. Versions of this discourse have been delivered to audiences in venues as odd and remote as Zagreb (to the Croatian Academy of Sciences), Novosibirsk (to a gathering of young academics, mainly philosophers), in Tokyo (again, to an academic gathering), and Addis Ababa (to the faculty and students of the Philosophy Department of the University). Lively discussions have always ensued, and it has been intriguing to see what aspect strikes home most with whom. In Zagreb, I was able, rather daringly, to adduce Marshal Tito as the one leader of modern times of whom I was aware who believed that no one should own more than five times anyone else, and this was confirmed to me by those who knew. In Novosibirsk, young people reacted rather strongly to the idea of national service, saying that they has just got free of the Komsomol, and they had no desire for any more of that sort of thing! I had to explain that this was really addressed rather to the democracies of

Western Europe. In Tokyo, people were concerned about the consequences of zero population growth, such as they are experiencing, and I had to agree that we in Europe face much the same problems, such as that of the funding of pensions, and what to do with the very elderly and infirm. The older generation also expressed worries about the insubordination of the young! Japanese society, it seems, is becoming less deferential and hierarchic, and this is disturbing to the older generation. In Addis, discussion centred, naturally, on where the developing world is expected to fit into this scenario. I emphasised that I was not opposed to all growth or development, but that I felt that, if anything, they could learn from our mistakes, and make a direct leap into an ecology-friendly system, using the energy sources which we are only now getting round to, and benefiting from our advances in technology.

The first edition has been sold out for some years now. I am much gratified that, through the noble initiative of Tim Addey and the Prometheus Trust, it can appear again, adorned with a most learned companion piece by my colleague Brendan O'Byrne, which serves to fill in much of the intellectual background to my remarks.

Platonism and the World Crisis

I

Let us start with the question of the radical imbalance currently prevailing between us and our environment. This is not, of course, just a problem of advanced Western civilisation, though it is a problem primarily caused by it. We are being joined in our aspiration for an affluent and wasteful lifestyle, in particular, by two enormous members of the emergent world, China and India, who, between them, have the capacity to sink the planet simply by seeking, as they have a perfect right to do, to emulate the material achievements of the chief Western powers, in particular the United States; while at the same time much of the so-called 'third world', particularly in sub-Saharan Africa, is engaged in a reckless proliferation of its population without exhibiting the slightest ability to support even its existing numbers.

At the root of our problems in this area over the last two hundred years or so is quite simply the modern concept of progress – that is to say, linear development upwards and outwards in all areas of society. We must build ever more roads, more houses, more public facilities; we must increase wealth – the Gross National Product – increase trade, exploit ever more fully all natural resources, vegetable, animal, and mineral. The inevitable increase in population consequent on that then necessitates further such 'development'. And all this is naively viewed as progress towards a happy and glorious future.

This concept of progress is so deeply ingrained in our psyches that it is hard for modern man to comprehend a culture in which no such concept is present. But such was the situation prevailing, so far as I know, in all pre-modern (let us say, pre-1600 A.D.) societies, and notably in the high civilisations of Greece and Rome, which, along with the Judaeo-Christian tradition, are our own direct ancestors.

Among Greek and Roman intellectuals, it was fully recognised that nations and societies had their ups and down, that empires rose and fell – and there may even be discerned, in the period of the high Roman Empire (notably the 2nd century AD) the notion that political arrangements, in the form of the *Pax Romana*, had attained a sort of apex, if not of perfection, then at least of satisfactoriness – but nowhere can we discern any trace of the modern obsession with 'progress'. On the contrary, it was universally accepted that change in the physical world was cyclical: some new inventions were made from time to time, predominantly in the area of warfare, populations might increase locally, and cities, such as Alexandria, Rome or Constantinople, grow to great size, communications, in the form of roads or safe passage on the sea, might improve marginally; but all this would be balanced by a decline somewhere else – none of these local developments was thought to be such as to disturb the overall cyclical nature of sublunar existence, especially as the life of the physical world, as it ceaselessly unrolled itself, was seen merely as a temporal projection of the eternal life of a higher, intelligible world, in which, of course, there was no question of change or development.

The nearest thing, I suppose, to an exception to this world-view was provided by thinkers in the early Christian tradition, who did indeed look forward to an end-time, the second Coming of Christ and the Day of Judgement, towards which all human life was working, a progression upon which Christ's first coming was an important milestone. This Christian scenario does indeed involve a concept of linear progress, albeit of a distinctly otherworldly variety, but it has been argued, and I think not without some plausibility, that it is this Christian concept, duly secularized and truncated of its culmination in a Last Judgement, that has spawned the modern concept of endless material progress.

For it is, after all, endless, and herein surely lies its inherent contradiction, and much of its perniciousness. Although all our material progress is notionally working towards some goal, this goal can logically never be attained. It must always be receding over the horizon, as it is an essential part of the dogma of modern capitalist development that a slow-down in the rate of growth is a disaster, as that is to be equated with *stagnation*, and stagnation is a very bad thing indeed, being next of kin to the ultimate misfortune, which is *recession*. So the Gross National Product has to keep on rising, and World Trade has got to keep on increasing, and the under-privileged hundreds of millions of China, India and elsewhere must continue to aspire to the ownership of motor-cars, second homes, computers, refrigerators, and video-recorders.

Most importantly, there can be no 'steady state' at the end of this rainbow. Every aspect of the economy must go on increasing exponentially. And herein lies the root of the crisis. Already we are seeing the disastrous results of global warming – a phenomenon in face of which the greatest polluter on the planet, the United States, is quite simply in a state of denial – most dramatically on sub-Saharan Africa, where desertification is spreading relentlessly, and at the two poles, where the icecaps are melting fast, but everywhere in recent years extremes of weather have been manifesting themselves, not least in the United States itself, with a succession of notable hurricanes. We are also seeing the initial steps in what is going to become an increasingly frantic battle for ever-shrinking oil resources – the preposterous and disastrous efforts to bring 'freedom and democracy', first to Afghanistan, and then to Iraq, being the opening shots, soon to be followed by devious intrigues among the corrupt regimes of Central Asia. And all this because our civilisation is, it seems, hopelessly hooked on the ever-increasing consumption of non-renewable fossil fuels.

At the same time as all this exponentially growing consumption is going on, we are faced also with the ever-increasing problem of the disposal of the waste matter generated by our life-style, some of it very toxic indeed, and all of it troublesome in one degree or another. Some years ago, a widely disseminated calculation estimated that the average middle-class American generates up to twenty-five times as much garbage as the average Indian or African villager, the average European not being far behind, and of course much more of that garbage is non-biodegradable. Admittedly, efforts are being made, much more seriously on the continent of Europe than either here in Ireland or in the US, to recycle as much of this as possible, but in this country in particular more or less every effort to re-process waste materials productively is met by ignorant or vexatious objections, and those by people who are generally every bit as productive of garbage as anyone else.

And that is only in relation to household rubbish. There is also the problem of commercial and medical waste, and beyond that the problem of the reckless pollution of rivers and lakes by farmers either ignorantly applying too much fertiliser to their fields, in search of ever-higher yields, or carelessly or dishonestly disposing of farmyard slurry. Everywhere one turns these days, one comes upon one aspect or another of the detritus of a culture expanding out of control.

So what does Plato, and the Platonist tradition, have to say about all this? What, one might wonder, could he possibly have to say? In fact, I want to propose to you that he has a great deal to say, and that we would do well to listen to him. I will take my examples primarily from his last work, *The Laws*, in which he presents us with his most serious sketch of an ideal state, but I will start from a passage in his more famous work, *The Republic* – also a sketch of an ideal state, but a far more peculiar one than that of *The Laws*, and one, I am convinced, that is not to be taken literally.

However, in Book II of *The Republic*, where he is engaged in a schematic account of the genesis of the state, he makes a particularly significant point when describing the transition from a primitive stage of society – which he portrays, with more than a touch of satire, as a kind of Golden Age utopia, in which small communities are living in complete harmony with their environments – to a more advanced stage, which he terms the 'pampered' or 'luxuryloving' state (*tryphôsa polis*) – or, more pointedly, the 'fevered' state (*phlegmainousa polis*). This is, of course, the situation in which all existing societies find themselves, and it comes about, he proposes (II 372Eff), as a result of the incessant desire to add luxuries to the necessities of life. To quote him:

> "There are some people, it appears, who will not be content with this sort of fare, or this sort of life-style (sc. of the primitive state); couches will have to be added, and tables and other furniture, yes, and relishes and myrrh and incense and courtesans and cakes – all sorts of all of them! And the items we first mentioned, houses and clothes and shoes, will no longer be confined to the level of the necessary, but we must introduce painting and embroidery, and procure gold and ivory and similar adornments, must we not?"

The consequence of this process of elaboration, as he goes on to point out, will be that the state will have to become bigger, and thus encroach on its neighbours (who will simultaneously be driven to encroach upon it), and the inevitable result of that will be that wars will break out, in the struggle to acquire more land and resources, or to protect trade routes – as ever-increasing foreign trade will follow necessarily from the demand for luxuries.

Is this not all, I would ask, though written in the middle of the fourth century BC, depressingly relevant to our present situation? We flatter ourselves that we have attained to a high degree of rationality and orderliness in our international relations, after the excesses of the past century in particular, but we must face the unpalatable fact that this thin façade of reasonableness will quickly break down if anyone dares to try to part us from our oil – as I say, the attempted 'liberation' of Iraq is only the first step in such a break-down; and such interventions as this will inevitably provoke ever more desperate and extreme responses from those who feel that they are being ruthlessly exploited, and have nothing to lose. And in the midst of all this mayhem, the oil itself, even making allowances for dramatic new discoveries in Central Asia and in Asiatic Russia, will inevitably run out in considerably less than a century from now. It is a limited, and non-renewable, resource.

So is there any solution to this problem? I am not at all sure that there is, but if there is, it has to be along the lines sketched out by Plato in his *Laws*. Now Plato is of course operating at a much simpler level than is appropriate for us, but, *mutatis mutandis*, I think that he can provide us with much food for thought. One of the first conditions that he establishes for his ideal state, in Book V of the work, is that its membership is to be strictly limited. This is easier to do, of course, when one is establishing a new colony, as he is, but the principle can be applied, broadly, to any state.

Let us take Ireland, for example. We in this country are in a rather interesting position in the modern world. We are a nation that, something over 150 years ago, had really far too many inhabitants for the resources available to support them – something over 8 million – and a dreadful famine was the result. I would not wish here to deny that British laissez-faire capitalism and plain indifference to Irish misery contributed to the dreadfulness, but the fact remains that the famine occurred because there were too many people for the available resources – and this is a situation being repeated in many parts of Africa, India and China today. However, in Ireland at the beginning of the 21st century, the situation is very different. After an initial halving of the population in the mid to late 19th century, and many decades of stagnation after that, our numbers are now rising, in response to the stimulus of unprecedented prosperity in the last decade of the 20th century, towards the 5 million mark. The question now arises, is there somewhere in here an ideal number of people to inhabit this green and pleasant land?

I have seen it stated, by responsible economists and demographers, that we probably could now support a population of something like the 8 million that pullulated here in misery in the early 1840s, and I don't doubt that they have a reasonable case. But, even if we granted that, the question arises, where do we stop? Are we to look forward then to 10 million? 15 million? After all, Holland, for instance, among our European neighbours, is about the size of Munster, and is now home to 16 million, and rising. Admittedly, they are Dutch – highly organised, very disciplined, used to living cheek-by-jowl – and we are... who we are, and used to a somewhat more chaotic and less crowded lifestyle; but still, the question may be raised.

I would like to answer the question, baldly and controversially, by proposing that an ideal population for us on this island would be just 5,040,000 – and I will now reveal why. Plato, in *Laws* V (737Dff.), declares that his ideal state, Magnesia, should consist of just 5040 households – that is to say, 5040 heads of household, with their wives and offspring, for a total citizen population of something like 20,000 – 25,000. This number – which is arrived at for amusing numerological reasons (it is divisible by all the numbers up to ten, and 59 ways in all!) – is truly tiny by modern standards, and need not be taken seriously in itself. What is significant about it is the ideological position that it represents. It lays down the principle of a 'steady-state' economy, of balance with the environment, and as such should be taken very seriously indeed. What Plato specifies is that the legislator should study the territory available very carefully, and determine as exactly as possible what number of people it could support 'in modest comfort', and then stick to that. It is central to his system that every citizen should have a basic stake in society, a land-holding that is inalienable and may not be subdivided: "the number of hearths established by the initial distribution must always remain the same; it must neither increase nor decrease. The best way for every state to ensure this will be as follows: the recipient of a holding should always leave from among his children only one heir to inherit his establishment. This will be his favourite son, who will succeed him and give due worship to the ancestors... of the family and state" (740B). The other children will be married off, if girls, or given out for adoption by childless households, if required – or else simply required to emigrate.

This is a stern arrangement – though something like that in fact prevailed unofficially in this country for many generations, God knows! – but there is a more positive aspect to it. Plato is above all concerned that no one in his society should fall below a certain level of modest prosperity; if they were to prove quite unable to run their allotment, they would simply be asked to leave the country (though every sort of advice and encouragement would be offered to them before that happened). Conversely, although Plato recognises the desirability of acknowledging different degrees of industriousness among the citizenry, and therefore allows some gradations in wealth, he is adamant that no one may be allowed to accumulate more than five times the basic property-valuation. Ancient Greeks did not think in terms of income, but rather of property, but if we were to transpose this principle into modern terms, we could say, as a rule of thumb, that, if the basic wage were fixed at, say, E20,000 then no one – doctor, lawyer, property speculator, or IT whiz-kid – for whatever reason, could be allowed to earn more than E100,000 per annum. If they wished to go beyond that, they would, once again, be asked to leave the country. As Plato puts it (744E-745A):

> "The legislator will use the holding as his unit of measure and allow a man to possess twice, thrice, and up to four times its value. If anyone acquires more than this, by finding treasure-trove or by gift or by a good stroke of business or some other similar lucky chance which presents him with more than he's allowed, he

should hand over the surplus to the state and its patron deities, thereby escaping punishment and gaining a good name for himself."

This, I must say, seems to me an excellent provision, much as it would disgust the contemporary neoconservative ideologists of capitalism. In modern terms, one would simply have to prescribe that anyone earning over five times the minimum wage would have the choice, and privilege, of donating his surplus to one of a number of approved public or private enterprises – I would naturally favour third-level education, but I recognise that there are many other very worthy causes out there! – or have the money removed from him by 100% taxation. It seems to me that society as a whole would be immensely the better for this, despite the frustration caused to a few. After all, as Plato remarks in the Republic, it is not our purpose to make any one class in the state happy, but rather the state as a whole.

I would certainly not wish to claim that Plato's vision of Magnesia is without flaws or defects. In particular, Plato exhibits a truly aristocratic disdain for anything approximating to 'trade' or industrial production, other than agriculture, in which we need not follow him. However, in his insistence on limiting such production (which in his ideal state would actually be performed by resident foreigners and/or slaves) to necessities rather than luxuries, and his insistence that, though there could be, no doubt, improvements in efficiency and effectiveness, there should be at all events no overall *growth*, I think that we should pay very serious attention to him. If his vision of a modest sufficiency of material goods sounds a little like that of Mr De Valera, in his famous St. Patrick's Day address of 1943, that is no accident; as political thinkers Plato and Dev had actually quite a lot in common. Let us take a passage of the *Laws* on the question of the possession of material wealth, and then append to that a portion of Dev's address. First Plato (743C-744A):

"The whole point of our legislation was to allow the citizens to live supremely happy lives in the greatest possible mutual friendship. However, they will never be friends if injuries and lawsuits arise amongst them on a grand scale, but only if they are trivial and rare. That is why we maintain that neither gold or silver should exist in the state, and there should not be much money made out of menial trades and charging interest... The citizens' wealth should be limited to the products of farming, and even here a man should not be able to make so much that he can't help forgetting the real reason why money was invented (I mean for the care of the soul and body, which without physical and cultural education respectively will never develop into anything worth mentioning). That's what has made us say more than once that the pursuit of money should come last in the scale of value. Every man directs his efforts to three things in all, and if his efforts are directed with a correct sense of priorities he will give money the third and lowest place, and his soul the highest, with his body coming somewhere between the two."

Now, as I say, we do not have to follow him in imposing a total ban on gold or silver money; let us focus rather on his scale of priorities. And now here is Dev:

"Let us turn aside for a moment to that ideal Ireland that we would have. That Ireland which we dreamed of would be the home of a people who valued material wealth only as the basis for right living, of a people who were satisfied with frugal comfort and devoted their leisure to the things of the spirit – a land whose countryside would be bright with cosy homesteads, whose fields and villages would be joyous with the sounds of industry, with the romping of sturdy children, the contests of athletic youths and the laughter of comely maidens, whose firesides would be forums for the wisdom of serene old age. It would, in a word, be the home of a people living the life that God desires that man should live."

It has in recent years become sadly customary, among the forward-thinking sophisticates of modern Ireland, to mock this speech – particularly, I suppose, the rompings of sturdy children, contests of athletic youths and the laughter of comely maidens (with which we may, I suppose, aptly contrast the proceedings every weekend nowadays in such venues as Temple Bar and elsewhere) – but I am inclined to salute it as an approximation to a noble vision. It is, at any rate, entirely in line with the vision of Plato.

What Plato, then, is presenting for our scrutiny is a strictly regulated 'steady-state' society, designed to secure both internal harmony by reason of the justice of its political and sociological arrangements, and harmony with its natural environment by ensuring that the demands it puts upon it do not exhaust or distort that environment. I should specify, in connexion with the former aim, that Plato placed enormous stress on education for citizenship (*paideia*), beginning from infancy, with the purpose of ensuring the full understanding of, and assent to, the principles on which the state was founded, on the part of the whole citizen body. In modern times, the United States goes some way towards this ideal – and of course the former Soviet Union and its satellites strove unsuccessfully to do so, as does China even now – but we in Europe have largely abdicated from any effort along these lines. Plato wanted above all, as did Benjamin Franklin and the other founders of the American Republic, an educated citizenry, any of whom could take on administrative responsibilities if necessary, but all of whom could at least make an informed judgement as to who among them was best qualified to rule, and vote accordingly. Indeed, so strongly did he feel on this point that anyone who proved unable or unwilling to exercise his citizenship was to be asked to leave the state altogether. There was no place in Magnesia for the 'Don't knows'!

To turn briefly to the problem of waste disposal: this is something on which Plato has really nothing to say, for the good reason that in the world as he knew it it was not a problem. The Classical Greeks were not necessarily a particularly tidy people – standards of hygiene in ancient cities would leave much to be desired from a modern perspective – but the fact was that most waste was thoroughly biodegradable and non-toxic, and did not pile up in such amounts as to constitute a crisis – dogs and birds could deal with most of it. What is left over is mostly the potsherds and metal utensils that give such delight to modern archaeologists; there were no indestructible plastics or radio-active residues to worry about. I think, however, that we can reasonably extrapolate from our knowledge of his philosophy in general so far as to say that he would have required that all the waste products of his ideal state should be recycled in one way or another – any pile-up of unusable garbage would inevitably indicate that society was no longer in harmony with its environment.

A further question might well occur to you, and it is one that I find a little awkward to answer, but answered it must be. It is all very well for Plato, you might say, to specify a fixed population of 5040 homesteads, and then say that all superfluous persons must simply leave; but how, in a modern democratic state, can one presume to set any sort of cap on population growth? The first reply I would make to that is to observe that it is in fact a feature of advanced western societies to limit their population growth spontaneously, to the extent that in Western Europe generally the indigenous population has attained something like steady state (with countries like Italy and Greece, - rather surprisingly – exhibiting a net decline); but nevertheless one must make provision for worst-case scenarios! If, as I feel would not be the case, population increase continued relentlessly, it would be necessary to take certain steps. One simple one would be to limit children's allowances to the first three children of any couple, instead of actually increasing them, as is currently the case. This would send out a pretty clear signal, I should think –

though of course stirring up indignation in certain quarters. A more extreme procedure would be – along Plato's own lines, but also borrowing a feature from the Kyoto Protocol on the production of greenhouse gases – that any children over the number of three produced by a given couple – or indeed a single mother – would have to be presented for adoption by childless couples, or at least those who had less than the maximum permitted number; or else the errant couple would actually have to 'buy' the variance to keep another child from some couple who had less than the specified number – very much as Ireland is currently having to pay up for generating too much carbon dioxide! And of course, parallel with all this, possibilities of immigration would have to be very strictly limited.

I realise, of course, that such provisions will strike many decent people as deeply shocking, but I would suggest to them in response that the situation that the human race as a whole currently faces is so serious that a seismic shift in our ethical consciousness will be necessary. It must come to seem (as I believe it is) deeply selfish and irresponsible, and hence positively *immoral*, to have more children than the environment can support, and such legislative provisions as I have outlined will only be expressing this sense of general disapproval. Morality, after all, is not a fixed quantity, much as religiously-minded people might like to think that it is; ethical positions shift in answer to changing societal circumstances – and it is quite reasonable that they should.

II

But that is, perhaps, enough about that for the moment! The second issue that I want to deal with is that of the clash of religious traditions, and religious intolerance in general. On the world stage, what we currently find ourselves faced with is the disastrous fact that, even as irrational and violent differences between the various

Christian sects have either faded away or are steadily lessening (except in such odd corners of the world as Northern Ireland!), the old antagonism between Christianity and Islam has taken on new and deadly forms. Of course, as we are constantly and correctly being reminded, this antagonism is not primarily fuelled by theological concerns – it is rather a response to the beastly treatment by the *Christian* United States' protegé Israel of its Palestinian neighbours, and more generally to the shock to Islamic morality inflicted by the gross vulgarity of Western (and again, largely American) popular culture, which floods in upon traditional Muslim societies through films, TV, music and glossy magazines. This is not to deny that Muslim society could do with some serious shocks, particularly in respect of its attitude to women, and to the treatment of criminals, but that does not lessen the force of the shocks inflicted, and this provokes a strong reaction, some of the results of which we are all too aware. We must add to these provocations the economic pressures of Western consumer society, which are also afflicting the majority of the inhabitants of Muslim nations, those who are not so fortunate as to belong to the Westernized elites who can enjoy the more positive aspects of consumerism. We saw, back in 1979, what could happen in a state such as Iran, and what in recent years has brought an (admittedly most moderate and circumspect) Islamist party to power in secular Turkey; and we should take due note of the pressures which are building up in such a society as Saudi Arabia.

However, all that said, the fact remains that this reaction is expressed in a distinctly religious mode, and it is the intransigent attitudes of both Christianity and Judaism that lends fuel to it. I speak with some feeling, as I have been recently browsing extensively in the Qur'an, and have come to see that, despite a good deal of polemic, Mohammed's revelation is deeply rooted in both Jewish and Christian thought. I myself would have considerable difficulty with the Prophet's prohibition on wine (which I believe was actually the result of rather local concerns, in the form of his objection to the use of wine in rituals honouring pagan goddesses in the region of Mecca), but in many other areas I feel that he has a lot to teach us. Primarily, though, Islam is traditionally much more tolerant of Judaism and Christianity than they have been of it. It sees itself, after all, as merely the culmination of a series of revelations which were made in earlier times to Abraham, to Moses, and to Jesus, and it incorporates much of what they had to say in its sacred text. The chief scandal and absurdity, from their point of view, is the claim by later Christians (though, they feel, not by Jesus himself) that he was, in some physical way, the *son* of God – and I must confess I find myself very much in agreement with them on that point. If the Christians could see their way to reformulating Jesus' status to that simply of a major prophet, and a man specially chosen and inspired by God, then, I think, the three great 'religions of the Book' could largely agree to differ on who delivered the most perfect and *final* revelation. The political and social pressures and sources of aggravation would continue, of course, but they would not be fuelled to the same extent by theological tensions.

But where, you may ask, does Plato and Platonism come into all this? Very significantly, I feel. Plato has an interesting attitude to established religion. On the one hand, as a legislator, he is most particular that the gods should be worshipped by the citizens of his state in the most conventional and traditional way. Atheism or irreverence he is prepared to punish most severely, as being profoundly subversive of morality. But he himself does not believe in the gods in their traditional forms, nor does he expect the wisest and most senior citizens in his ideal state to do so; and this attitude of his (which was in fact, it must be admitted, by no means unique to him among the intellectuals of Classical Athens) communicated itself to his successors, in the form of a tradition of allegorizing religious symbols and myths.

In his early dialogue *Euthyphro*, Plato makes his mentor Socrates probe mercilessly the theological assumptions of the pompous Euthyphro, who is actually representing, albeit in an extreme form, the beliefs of the Athenian people in general. It is plain from Socrates' questions that he does not accept the traditional myths about the gods, their amours, their other interventions in the human world, and their quarrels among themselves. Later, in Book II of the *Republic* (378Aff.), Plato makes Socrates lay down a set of rules about how to talk about the gods, which once again indicates Plato's rejection of traditional mythology. The gods, or God – Plato is quite happy to talk about 'God' (*ho theos*) in the singular – must not be described as doing any harm to, or perpetrating any deception upon, men; God is entirely good, and eternally unchanging. This effectively takes care of the great bulk of Greek traditional theology, which Socrates proceeds to take apart.

And yet in the *Republic*, and more clearly still in the *Laws*, Plato insists on scrupulous religious observance in his ideal state. The traditional gods of the Olympian pantheon, though stripped of all unsuitable stories about them, are to be worshipped in the traditional manner, and so are a host of lesser divinities, daemons, heroes and even nymphs. In Book V of the *Laws* (738Cf.), he insists that all traditional ceremonies and sacrifices should be performed, and that all the citizens should attend the festivals. There is to be a full set of temples on the acropolis of the central town, and other precincts of the gods in each of the twelve divisions into which the state is divided (745Bff.).

How are we to reconcile these positions? Is Plato being simply disingenuous, and promoting traditional religion as something like an 'opium of the people? Well, I think that one would have to admit that he is not being entirely straightforward, but he is not being hypocritical either. He would reconcile these two positions by the application of allegorical exegesis. In Book X of the same *Laws*, after

gaining power by showing skill at winning over or subduing the owner, and describe him as an accomplished seaman, a true captain, a naval expert; but they criticise anyone different as useless. They completely fail to understand that any genuine sea-captain has to study the yearly cycle, the seasons, the heavens, the stars and winds, and everything relevant to the job, if he's to be properly equipped to hold a position of authority in a ship. In fact, they think it's impossible to study and acquire expertise at how to steer a ship (leaving aside the question of whether or not people want you to) and at the same time be a good captain." (trans. Robin Waterfield).

Well, we get the message, I think. The ship-owner is the State, or the Sovereign People, and the crew members are the democratic politicians and ideologues. Much of his criticism, I feel, is applicable to our own situation, as much as to that of Classical Athens. We too hold in theory to the democratic creed that any citizen is *ipso facto* capable of rule, and that that requires no particular degree of expertise - though in practice we recognise that the details of government now have become so abstruse that there is need of a highly-trained civil service and a host of (highly-paid) advisers and consultants on top of that, to manage the politicians and set them right.

Plato, on the contrary, maintains that ruling is a science, and indeed the master science, and that perfection in it requires years of training. In the ideal state portrayed in the *Republic*, which is what is familiar to most people who know anything about him, this results in the rule of a small elite of so-called 'philosopher-kings', presiding over a large standing army-cum-police force, and a much larger proletariate of artisans and farmers, who constitute the productive element in the state, but who wield no power whatsoever.

I am always surprised, though, that this arrangement is taken seriously as a political blueprint by so many scholars who should know better, as well as by the general public. For me, the problem with it is this. It runs counter to one principle which was basic to Plato's political philosophy, and which he inherited from Socrates (it features in the *Apology*, which is Socrates' speech from the dock, as well as in the *Laws*), so that it cannot be dismissed as just something that he developed in his old age: the principle that any well-run state requires the *educated assent* of all the citizens, and this in turn requires that they *all* undergo the same *paideia*, or moral and intellectual training. This training is something that the lowest and largest class in the *Republic* conspicuously lacks – indeed, if the scenario presented is pressed to its logical conclusion, they do not even possess the brain to absorb such a training. In fact, what Plato is doing in the *Republic* is taking the opportunity to air a number of his cherished political ideas, while primarily presenting a schema of the well-ordered human soul, in which the reasoning element corresponds to the philosopher-kings, the spirited element to the soldiery, and the passionate element to the artisan class. The passionate element in the soul is essentially irrational, and must be subdued initially by force, though in a well-ordered soul it can come, like a well-trained and obedient dog, to assent to its being ruled, though without ever attaining full understanding of the whys and wherefores of that.

In the *Laws* – where he is being serious about constructing a state – we find a very different situation. Every citizen of the state, male and (to some extent, at least) female, is assumed to have been subjected to the same comprehensive education – beginning not just in infancy, but even in the womb (Plato was a great believer in antenatal exercises [cf. VII 788A-790A], to instil a sense of harmony into the unborn infant!) – which, while covering the basic skills of reading, writing and arithmetic, is primarily concerned with instilling right attitudes – young people are to learn, from their earliest years, to love and hate the right things (653A-C):

"I maintain that the earliest sensations that a child feels in infancy are of pleasure and pain, and this is the route by which virtue and vice first enter the soul… I call 'education' the initial acquisition of virtue by the child, when the feelings of pleasure and affection, pain and hatred, that well up in his soul are channelled in the right courses before he can understand the reason why. Then when he does understand, his reason and his emotions agree in telling him that he has been properly trained by inculcation of appropriate habits. Virtue is this general concord of reason and emotion. But there is one element you could isolate in any account you give, and this is the correct formation of our feelings of pleasure and pain, which makes us hate what we ought to hate from first to last, and love what we ought to love. Call this 'education', and I, at any rate, think you would be giving it its proper name."

Now this, we might say, is outright 'brain-washing', and we might appear at first sight to have a point, but I think that we should be less free than we are in the use of that term. The aim of 'brain-washing' techniques, after all, is to scrub from the brain a set of existing beliefs, and to produce a sort of zombie in place of a reasoning being. Plato is concerned to inculcate right beliefs in brains which have not yet acquired any, and he would make no apology for that. It was his view that young persons should be set firmly on the right road, morally and intellectually, by their elders – and when they in turn come into the full possession of their reason, they will reflect rationally on their education, and see that it was the right one, and be duly grateful.

Now we in the western world are, not unreasonably, pretty uncomfortable these days about the inculcation of 'values' into the young – the whole process smacks of authoritarianism of one sort or another, religious or secular – and yet we do, I think, often wish that they had some values. Our position, I would argue, is in fact deeply incoherent, where Plato's is coherent. We feel that there should be *some* instruction in schools concerning ethical principles and the duties of citizenship, but we have great difficulty in deciding just what that should be like. Is one, for instance, to have totally value-free, 'non-judgemental', sex education, or should one throw in some recommendations against reckless promiscuity and in favour of treating people as whole persons, rather than as mere sex-objects? And how about standards of honesty and public-spiritedness, when dealing with one another or with the state? Then, we are most uncomfortable in general about censorship of books and films, but we draw the line at child pornography and the stirring-up of racial hatred. And then we get very hot under the collar, and enact strict regulations, about smoking and drug-taking, but we simply wring our hands when faced with excessive drinking of alcohol or ingestion of junk foods. A censorious outsider, such as Plato – or indeed some relic from the former socialist countries – might conclude that we have simply lost our nerve, and are floundering around from case from case.

I must confess that I have come to the conclusion, in my old age, that modern western society is going to have to tighten itself up, on various fronts, if we are to avert a serious breakdown of civil society. If we do not take the proper steps voluntarily, I would predict a series of outrages in the areas of morality and public order, which, like '9-11', will produce a convulsive over-reaction, and we will wake up one morning to find ourselves under a dictatorship far more unpleasant than anything that I am advocating.

So what am I advocating? Well, the single biggest innovation that I would propose is a system of National Service, and by that I mean something truly worthy of that name – not just a euphemism for military service (though I would have no objection to the imposition of military discipline during such a period!). It seems to me that our greatest failure as a society in modern times is to develop a mechanism for initiating young persons into adult life, a life of responsible citizenship, such as is more or less universal in more traditional societies, and was in place even in democratic Athens. The period from eighteen to twenty is one of great stress in most young people's lives, and it here that a regime of strict, though rational, order might most advantageously be imposed. This would, of course, involve considerable initial cost, but the savings in the avoidance of anti-social behaviour and blighted lives, as well as the various worthy public work projects that the young people would be set to work on, would amply compensate for this in the longer run.

Should such an institution be compulsory? Probably, but one alternative that occurs to me would be simply to make it clear that, if one declined to take part, one would henceforth no longer be considered a full citizen of the state, for the purpose of receiving any benefits, such as health services, higher education, unemployment benefit or old age pension. That should settle the matter for most 'conscientious objectors'. I do not see that this is unduly harsh. Claims for rights must be balanced by a recognition of duties, and that lesson cannot be learned too early.

At any rate, during the eighteen months or two years of service, young people, besides experiencing strict (but rational and humane) discipline and order, and performing useful physical labour, would attend lectures on the history and structure of the state, and on ethical and political theory. This sounds pretty heavy stuff for many young persons, but these subjects could be made lively and attractive with some thought and suitable packaging.

In Book VI of the *Laws* (760-1), Plato sketches out some of the tasks that he envisages for those on his variety of National Service. There are a number of defence-related tasks that need not concern us, but he then continues:

"The rain that God sends must do the countryside good, not harm, so the country-wardens (his name for those on National Service) must see that the water flowing off the high ground down into any sufficiently deep ravines between the hills is collected by dikes and ditches, so that the ravines can retain and absorb it, and supply streams and springs for all the districts of the countryside below, and give even the driest of spots a copious supply of pure water.

As for water that springs from the ground, the wardens must beautify the fountains and rivers that form by adorning them with trees and buildings; they must use drains to tap the individual streams and collect an abundant supply, and any grove or sacred enclosure which has been dedicated nearby must be embellished by having a perennial flow of water directed by irrigation into the very temples of the Gods.

The young men should erect in every quarter gymnasia for themselves and senior citizens, construct warm baths for the old folk, and lay up a large stock of thoroughly dry wood. All this will help to relieve invalids, and farmers wearied by the labour of the fields – and it will be a much kinder treatment than the tender mercies of some fool of a doctor!"

Whatever about this last remark, these provisions embody very much what I would envisage for the activities of those on National Service: care for the environment, beautification of the countryside, and care for the disabled and elderly.

And not only would I prescribe this basic period of National Service: I would advocate that, as is the practice in Switzerland, for instance, at the present time, all adults should be encouraged to return to the system for a period of a week or two every year up to at least the age of sixty, and that they should be given time off from their work to do this, over and above their normal holiday allowance. I think that this would prove a very salutary 'topping-up' of the good practices that they had developed during their original service. It would be a tonic for both body and mind!

This, then, I would see as one key development, if one wished to restructure the state along more Platonic lines. I say *more* Platonic, as I would not for a moment advocate a full dose of Platonism for a modern state, even if there were any prospect of a modern state being prepared to take it. The degree of planning and control of citizens' lives which Plato advocates is something that I for one would find quite intolerable, and I am sure that this would be the general reaction. It is only the basic premiss of Plato's political philosophy that I feel we have something to learn from, and that is that it is the right and duty of a state, not only to provide a life for its citizens, but a *good* life, in the sense of a virtuous and purposeful life. And since states cannot do their own providing, being abstract entities, this has to translate into a consensus, however arrived at, of the citizens over thirty – that is to say, the dominant generation. It is they, I should say, who have the right, and the duty, to prescribe codes of conduct, and subjects of study, for the younger generation, including, of course, their own children. If this dominant generation loses its nerve – as I must say I saw it doing in the America of the 1960s – then society as a whole begins to fall apart. When I arrived in Berkeley, California, in 1966, the slogan going around was 'Don't trust anyone over thirty!' In a well-run society, I would suggest, this slogan should be virtually reversed: 'Don't entrust any important decision-making to anyone under thirty!'

If the principle of a period of National Service were accepted, I think that all else that is necessary would follow from that. Firstly, a sense of discipline and purposiveness would be projected downwards, throughout the school system; and secondly, the influence of the institution would progressively filter upwards throughout the state, as cohort after cohort graduated, and took their place in society. A spin-off of this would, I hope, be an enhanced respect – duly earned, one hopes! – for those in public office or other positions of authority, and a willingness to attribute the highest motives rather than the lowest to them, unless proved otherwise.

That is all I have to say on my third chosen topic. I realise that, on all three of these topics, which seem to me more or less the salient features of the crisis which is facing Western civilisation in particular, but also the world in general, I have been driven to utter many hard sayings, and some things that may appear shocking to some sensibilities. What I have tried to do, though, is to apply principles that I discern in Plato, and the tradition that originates with him, to the world in which we live, to see if he might have anything to offer us. I have deliberately confined myself on this occasion to his political thought. Another essay, on another occasion, might concern itself rather with his metaphysics, his belief in another realm of existence superior to this physical one, a realm of the spirit, where the purified soul may contemplate eternal truths without the interference of the body. But Plato himself is first of all a deeply political philosopher. His first priority is to get the *environment* right, to establish a state in which rational life and discourse can flourish. And that is what I have been concerned with on this occasion.

The Urgency of Platonism: the Philosophical Background to the World Crisis

Brendan O'Byrne

In an essay entitled 'The Age of the World Picture', the philosopher Martin Heidegger said this about the nature of metaphysics and its relation to an epoch:

> "Metaphysics grounds an age in that, through a particular interpretation of beings and through a particular comprehension of truth, it provides that age with the ground of its essential shape. This ground comprehensively governs all decisions distinctive of the age. Conversely, in order for there to be adequate reflection on these phenomena, their metaphysical ground must allow itself to be recognised in them." [1]

On this account, we could gain an essential understanding of our own age if we were to grasp its distinctive conception of being and truth. What we can certainly say at this point is that the metaphysic of our age is decidedly un-Platonic.[2]

---

[1] 'The Age of the World Picture' in Martin Heidegger *Off the Beaten Track* Julian Young & Kenneth Haynes (trr & edd.) Cambridge University Press, 2002: p 57.

[2] Any attempt to give a detailed definition of the term Platonic seems doomed to failure on account of the great heterogeneity within the tradition that takes that name. In view of these difficulties I propose a minimalist definition which will serves us well if it does nothing else than set out an opposition to the distinctive metaphysic of the present age. I take the distinctive hallmark of Platonism to be a realist metaphysic that explains reality by reference to an ultimate immaterial first principle upon which beings are mediately or immediately contingent, *i e* the Idea of the Good as described in Plato's *Republic*. See also Lloyd Gerson *Aristotle and Other*

In 2006 The Dublin Centre for the Study of the Platonic Tradition, under the direction of Prof John Dillon, instituted a series of public lectures, delivered by some prominent Irish intellectual figures of unconventional outlook, under the series title 'Platonism and the World Crisis'. Dillon set the theme with a lecture under that very title which was later published as a pamphlet (so far 3 of the 5 lectures given to date have been published in pamphlet form).[3] This series was based on the assumption that the modern world really is in crisis and that we ought to set about diagnosing this crisis and discussing possible solutions and alternative ways of being and doing.

In the lecture, 'Platonism and the World Crisis', Dillon set about the task of looking at the modern world through Platonic spectacles. He selected three topics on which to focus and which he described as representing "the great bulk of what is wrong with modern western society, and what is inexorably putting intelligent life on this planet under mortal threat."

These he lists as follows:

1. The problem of the destruction of the environment and of waste disposal.
2. The problem of religious conflict and mutual intolerance.
3. The problem of the legitimation of authority and the limits of personal freedom.

Now someone might take issue with this schema on any number of grounds – they might even deny there is a crisis in the sense described and even maintain that things have never been better. Whatever about all that, my assumption here is that there is indeed a

---

Platonists Cornell University Press, 2005 ch 1 'What is Platonism?' for a seven point definition which is as good as any we might come up with.

[3] John Dillon *Platonism and the World Crisis* Dublin Centre for the Study of the Platonic Tradition, 2007.

serious crisis and malaise affecting western civilisation and that it runs very deep.[4] If we attend closely to each item of the three set out by Dillon, we may notice that it somewhat resembles the ancient philosophical division of things by subject matter. The first deals with our relationship with nature; the second points to our most fundamental conceptions of reality (whilst also invoking the spectre of moral relativism); and the third looks at ourselves and our relationships with each other; that is, how one ought to live, and, the kinds of formal structures that ought to shape the way we live as part of a community or society.

Having looked at various kinds of problems under these headings, Dillon goes on to suggest some solutions that Plato or a Platonist might have suggested towards their resolution. Herein lies the special interest of this text. Instead of expanding on the prescriptive aspects, I would like to supplement his account by looking at these issues from a somewhat different perspective.

What I propose to do here is two things. The first is to make some preliminary remarks about the philosophical background to the kinds of developments that have led to this crisis described under Dillon's threefold division, and secondly, to examine all this through a Platonic lens. Beginning with the first, if we turn to the phenomenon of environmental destruction, we really ought to consider the origin of the kind of *thinking* that leads people to view a forest of trees as just so many million cubic metres of timber, as opposed, say, to a lush and somewhat mysterious and enchanting natural locale which can sustain a diversity of life, or, as a unique *place* that enters into the topographic lore of a people. One calls to mind here the place that Sherwood Forest occupies in the collective imagination of the English people, as the *topos* of the marvellous and heroic exploits of Robin

---

[4] The present world order is essentially western in origin in all essential respects. Therefore the world crisis is a crisis of western civilisation.

Hood and his Merry Men as preserved in popular tradition.[5] So how did we end up in a metaphysical dispensation that dismisses this kind of attitude to forests as just so much superstition and sentimentality and instead views the world around us as little more than a complex mass of "resources" for our systematic exploitation?

Turning to the second item, I do not propose to address the specific question of religious conflict *per se*, for this is not a peculiarly modern problem; however, I do want to look briefly at the background to some contemporary tensions whereby we find a proliferation of often mutually exclusive and sometimes hostile world-views within the same society, and that lead to the kinds of fragmentation that underlie the kinds of conflicts Dillon discusses.[6] We may think of examples here, such as the intensely bitter and divisive issue that is the contemporary abortion debate or the equally fraught question surrounding state recognition of same-sex unions. Sometimes these seemingly irreconcilable divisions erupt into violence; recall the appalling atrocities of a few years ago when the public transport system of London was so wickedly attacked with great loss of life. How *did* we get to a situation where we now inhabit a veritable Babel of radically opposed moral view-points which biliously simmer away, sometimes even exploding into violence?

Under the third category I also propose to discuss the philosophical background to what one contemporary political philosopher, Jurgen Habermas, calls the "legitimation crisis."[7] It seems that in the modern

---

[5] Of course even here, there is a process of disenchantment at work. Sober scientific historiography will tell us that Hood was not quite the populist hero revered in folk memory.

[6] For a discussion of the background to the Babel of contemporary moral discourse see Alisdair MacIntyre's *After Virtue* especially ch 2 on the mutual incomprehension which characterises much contemporary moral debate.

[7] Jurgem Habermas, *Legitimation Crisis* (tr Thomas McCarthy) Boston: Beacon Press, 1975.

world, when one searches for the ground and source of legitimacy for authority, one tends to come up against a blank wall. On the one hand we are referred to the "will of the people", on the other, to time-honoured customs and institutions which are often opaque in their origins. It seems difficult to find a coherent set of arguments that can bind our inner loyalty to the modern state and other institutions. The liberal state privileges the private sphere over the public and yet, equally, it makes great demands on modern citizens in the name of the *greater*, public good. Seeming contradictions such as this do not make the search for legitimacy any easier, especially if it turns out that what *seem* to be contradictions in the liberal state turn out to be very real.

Now, the second thing I want to do is to examine these themes through a Platonic lens. In fact I want to suggest that some, if not all, of these problems arise from certain basic theses that are already critically examined in the dialogues of Plato, notably the claims made so forcefully on behalf of *pleonexia* and defended by the character of Callicles in the *Gorgias*[8]; or the view that right and wrong is reducible to the existing customs of society, a view defended by Protagoras in the eponymous dialogue and which is usually termed moral relativism, and, a view that is described in a later dialogue, the *Sophist*, that the criterion of being is body, classic materialism, a view that is today known as metaphysical naturalism, and which has become, or is still in the process of becoming, the default metaphysic of our age.[9]

[8] Lit *wanting more than one's share*; Callicles uses the term to denote a life based on appetite satisfaction.
[9] The view that all that is is body is the position held by the Giants in what is described as the *gigantomachia peri tes ousias*, 'the battle of the Gods and the Giants over being.' Naturalism so described has made serious inroads into academic philosophy departments in the last few decades.

The thesis that I wish to advance, at least in a preliminary and sketchy form, given the restrictions of space, is as follows: modern science and political liberalism largely form the basis of the modern world and have their source in a series of interconnected theses which have already been sharply criticised by Plato in various dialogues and which are ultimately ethical in their origin and their implications. I will term this *political hedonism*.[10]

The modern world represents the triumph of a particular answer to the fundamental ethical question: how ought one to live, and, by extension, how ought we to live *together*? The ethical position here derives in large part from a revived but debased form of Epicureanism. Ethical hedonism is fiercely opposed in the Platonic dialogues as it is completely antithetical to Platonism. It is the belief that the good life consists in the maximisation of pleasure and the minimisation of pain which will result in *ataraxia*, or the calm inner peace that comes from complete detachment from worldly cares.[11]

Pleasure here does not mean Bacchanalian excess or physical enervations epitomised by the life-style of the gourmand or the libertine; in fact Epicurus was a rather ascetic character himself and the personal discipline (*askesis*) of his school was as demanding as

[10] The phrase is Leo Strauss's and he used it to describe Hobbes: "Political atheism and political hedonism belong together. They arose together in the same mind [Hobbes] at the same time." *Natural Right and History* University of Chicago Press: Chicago, 1965 pb edition, p 196.

[11] Modern Epicureanism differs radically from its ancient form in that the difference between necessary and unnecessary desires, held strictly apart by Epicurus, is collapsed, for the asceticism demanded of authentic Epicureanism is deemed unrealisable by the masses; therefore the classical virtues as the means towards *eudaimonia* (happiness or human fulfilment) are abolished. Henceforth the basis of civil society is no longer the pursuit of excellence (*arete*, virtue) but is now simply the pursuit of 'commodious living', *commoda hujus vitae*. See Strauss, *NRH*, p 188-9. For commodious living we can substitute consumerism as a hedonic utilitarian doctrine, i e greatest good for the greatest number, where the good equals the pleasant.

any other. Pleasure-pain in this view simply means the absence of enervations or stimuli, such as to distract one from the ultimate aim of achieving a tranquillity born of detachment (*ataraxia*), a kind of inner peace which comes as a result of a successful withdrawal from the trials and tribulations of life.

One of the other significant differences between ancient hedonism and its modern incarnation, which is alluded to above, centres on the political realm. The ancient Epicureans disavowed public life, preferring withdrawal into the private sphere, for politics causes great stress and turmoil to its practitioner, inhibiting the development of tranquil detachment (*ataraxia*), whereas modern hedonism, in stark contrast, is actually a political project. If the aim of modern neo-Epicureanism is simply to attain commodious living rather than the cultivation of the virtues as a means to inner detachment, as with ancient Epicureanism, then the inhibition on political praxis is removed — in fact it is necessitated. Private life is privileged over public but, paradoxically, the neo-Epicurean is forced into public life simply to secure and maintain the primacy of the private sphere! This is the essential aim of liberal politics.

In the middle ages, there was no direct knowledge of Epicureanism — instead they understood it only through highly pejorative and essentially false reports of libertinage and excess transmitted largely from Patristic sources.[12] The first rediscovery of first-hand Epicurean testimony occurred when Poggio Bracciolini discovered a manuscript of Lucretius in 1417 which was first printed in 1473, while commentaries started to appear from 1511. This was supplemented by the growing availability of Diogenes Laertius' *Lives of the*

---

[12] Ancient hostility to Epicureanism revolved solely around its political irresponsibility with the additional objection to its materialism made by the Platonists. The Stoics were also materialists but took an opposite view of political responsibility.

Philosophers. The rediscovery of Epicurean texts paved the way for an Early Modern Epicurean revival, culminating with such figures as Pierre Gassendi, who attempted the highly implausible project of synthesising Epicureanism and Christianity, and also Francis Bacon, philosopher and Lord Chancellor of England. Francis Bacon was an Epicurean in both the philosophical sense but also in the pejorative sense, whilst Descartes, as one scholar points out, is "very careful in several letters to point out that his moral notions are a development of and expansion upon both Stoicism and Epicureanism, uniquely fashioned by his metaphysical notions."[13] By the seventeenth century, Epicurean doctrines were firmly embedded into the intellectual life of western Christendom. With this in mind, I want to take Francis Bacon and René Descartes as the emblematic founders of the modern world both in its scientific and ethico-political sense. Later on I will add Thomas Hobbes to this line-up.

To conclude this section, I want to end with a quote from Agnes Heller's classic work *Renaissance Man* which seems to capture and summarise the intellectual and spiritual situation of the early modern period, especially in the way that the different schools of ancient materialism are conflated and then distilled into a basic attitude or orientation. Early modern Epicureanism is not so much a set of doctrines but a metaphysical mood which suffuses every aspect of the modernising movement:

> Little by little stoicism and epicureanism abandoned those differences of detail, often significant in their day, which had characterised them during antiquity. Detached from speculations relating to the philosophy of nature (atomism, the theory of universal conflagration), from fatalism and the aristocratic attitude that necessarily went with it, stoicism and

[13] Vance G Morgan *Foundations of Cartesian Ethics* (Humanities Press) New Jersey, 1994: p 132 n 25.

epicureanism finally merged. The process of fusion was already discernible during the Renaissance, although it was completed only at the end of the period.

Thus modern stoicism (or epicureanism) was far from being a concrete philosophy any longer, much less a philosophical system; it had become a basic attitude towards reality or an ethically tinged form of conduct, which might go together with quite different philosophical systems – though not, of course, with any and all philosophical systems. Still, it always retained a certain ontological foundation, in the absence of which the basic attitude could never have arisen.[14]

The essence of modern science

The orthodox view that not only pervades the academy but enjoys popular acclaim goes something like this. Science is a pure and disinterested activity that aims at gaining as much reliable knowledge about the world as possible. Modern science is superior to pre-modern science – Newton's theory of gravity is *true* whereas Aristotle's theory of two kinds of motion is *false*. Science not only affords us *reliable* knowledge of the world but also by dint of this very reliability, it shapes our practical attempts to interact with nature through the forms of technology. Technology draws on modern science. Modern science arises in the 17th century whereas modern technology begins in the 18th. Modern science is both essentially and chronologically prior to modern technology.

This pretty much summarises the popular view about science and technology and their mutual relationship. However, I believe this broad and interconnected panoply of views is untenable. Instead, I

[14] Agnes Heller *Renaissance Man* Schoken Books, New York: 1982 pp 105-106.

think it can be shown that modern science is *technological* in its essence, a thesis originally set out by Martin Heidegger and which is a thesis which can be supported with testimony from the early modern natural philosophers themselves.[15]   Far from being disinterested, modern science is motivated by a now long-running project that aims at subduing and manipulating nature to ends posited through human willing.   The behavioural psychologist B F Skinner famously described modern science as simply "prediction and control."   This is very far from any notion of disinterested observation.   Modern science is primarily and originally about the manipulation of nature.   Hans Blumenberg, who himself affirms the legitimacy of the modern world, perceptively observes in his magnum opus *The Legitimacy of the Modern Age*, that the modern world's legitimacy is located in the self-assertion of the will.   But then a Platonist would say that this – the self-assertion of the will - is precisely what de-legitimises it![16]

All the early modern scientists, or natural philosophers as they described themselves, subscribed to a technological and purely instrumental conception of science.   Francis Bacon famously said that he considered nothing worthy of being called truth that was not also useful.   Contrast this with the view of Aristotle, who was the epitome of everything Bacon despised.[17]   The first line of the *Metaphysics*

---

[15] Martin Heidegger, 'The Question Concerning Technology' in *The Question Concerning Technology and Other Essays* (tr William Lovitt) Harper & Row: New York, 1977.   For a fuller discussion of this see Trish Glazebrook *Heidegger's Philosophy of Science* Fordham University Press: New York, 2000, and, Richard Rojcewicz *The Gods and Technology: A Reading Of Heidegger* SUNY Press: Albany, 2006.

[16] This modern day Prometheanism is what Oswald Spengler, an early exponent of the western crisis thesis, termed Faustian.

[17] Although in his more sober assessments, 'Aristotle' is simply a cover-all term for the dominant scholastic philosophy which was largely derived from Aristotle and adapted for Christian use.   Bacon's less polemicised views of Aristotle (and Plato) are more measured.

begins, 'man of his nature *loves* to know', whilst elsewhere he states that the highest life possible for man is the *bios theoretikos*, the life of contemplation of immutable entities and relations. For Aristotle, in sharp contrast to Bacon, wisdom is sought for its own sake – it is the way in which we come to model ourselves on the divine. Wisdom is not useful knowledge of the workings of nature but a grasp of the basic principles of reality, ultimately of the divine. Aristotle's God, as we learn from Book XII of his *Metaphysics*, is the pure activity of self-contemplation, *noesis noesios noesis* (lit thinking thinking about thinking). Philosophy, on this view, is the means by which we draw closer to the divine in this imitative way. This is really not essentially different from something Socrates says in the *Theaetetus*: that the purpose of life is "to become like God as much as is possible for us" (*Theaet* 176a).

Bacon proposes a wholesale reform of knowledge beginning with a new ideal; that of usefulness for ameliorating man's physical condition. This can and will be brought about through the mastery of nature. The mastery of nature can only come about if the scientist attends to the workings of nature through observation and thereby gains knowledge of its workings. Through this knowledge and *only* though this knowledge, can mastery be achieved. It was Bacon who said: "Knowledge is power.—*Nam et ipsa scientia potestas est*" and the dedication of *The Advancement of Learning* reads: "For the glory of the Creator and the relief of man's estate." Knowledge as power is no more than an early formulation of Skinner's prediction-control model of science. The practical business of this new knowledge would have to be a corporate undertaking requiring coordination and direction with research being broken up according to the nature of each object of investigation and brought under directed teams of researchers. To this end Bacon conceived of what is in essence the modern university as research institute dedicated to accumulating new knowledge of a useful kind.

Bacon was surely right when he realised that if the new science was to succeed, it had to be a corporate undertaking within a politically directed hierarchy which begins at the base with the individual researcher, rising through the divisions according to object, leading right up to the apex of the pyramid in office of Lord Chancellor. He was also correct to perceive that this had to be a trans-historical project; the mastery of nature would not be complete within a generation or even a couple of generations, but would in fact turn out to be an open-ended, cumulative affair, and as such, forms much of the substance of the concept of progress. He was also acutely aware – as were Descartes and all the other modernists - that the reigning metaphysical-cosmological paradigm had to be overcome and replaced. This comes out in his frequent and intemperate tirades against Aristotle and theoretical philosophy in general. Descartes too, in his letters to Mersenne, speaks in confidence to his friend about the need to speak past the schoolmen in a veiled way, which will be understood by those who are open to and welcoming of this fundamental shift.[18]

With all this a new guiding notion enters into historical determination which has led to the well-known secularisation thesis advanced by intellectual historians, although this is contested by some, notably the intellectual historian Hans Blumenberg.[19] According to this thesis, the notion of progress represents a secularisation of the Christian promise of eternal salvation and final judgement. Under this view, human history is first endowed with future directed *meaning*. In antiquity there was no real concept of progress, and history was understood as cyclical, in harmony with

[18] Letter to Mersenne of January 28, 1641, cited in Charles Larmore, 'Descartes and Skepticism' in ed Stephen Gaukroger *The Blackwell Guide to Descartes' Meditations* Oxford, 2006: 17-29.

[19] Hans Blumenberg *The Legitimacy of the Modern Age* (1966).

the cyclical cosmology.[20]   With the advent of Christ linearity enters into the world; the circle is broken, as it were, and straightened out into a line. A substantial difference in cosmology obtains between the world before Christ and the world after from a cyclical to an eschatological model. History henceforth becomes ends-directed.

The early Church soon advocates a doctrine whereby Christ will return once again only this time, not as a humble carpenter, but as king of the universe come to give final judgement over all souls and on human history. The very first generation believed this return to be immanent such that they would not have even have to undergo a physical death, it would occur in their lifetime. But as they died off and this return was not in evidence, it was pushed into some unspecified future until eventually it is situated in some very far and notional future. Nonetheless, henceforth the passing of each moment brings us closer to this event, that is, to the consummation of the world, its fulfilment and perfection in the resurrection of the dead and the final judgement. That each moment brings us closer to that final moment could be understood as the first appearance of the idea of progress, properly speaking, and an accompanying sacralisation of history as fully meaningful. But this kind of progress is exclusively Christological and messianic and is solely focussed on soteriological and eschatological ends.

Now if we are to remove the religious or "supernatural" element in all this we are left with a notion of progress as such, but now *this* progress is to be measured by the accumulation of *useful* knowledge leading to a steady unfolding of the project of bringing nature under human mastery, that is, better and more refined instruments and

---

[20] On the absence of anything like the modern notion of progress in antiquity see, E R Dodds, *The Ancient Concept of Progress and Other Essays on Greek Literature and Belief* Oxford, 1973.

techniques. Instead of a movement towards the Kingdom of Christ on earth, we are now supposedly progressing towards an ever greater future society which takes on a distinctly utopic character – futurologists tend to engage in utopian projections, the optimistic ones, that is.[21] Progress also introduces *qualitativeness* into the passage of time. As time goes past we are drawing ever nearer towards the utopia such that when we look back we see something of lesser value because it is less developed or less progressed. On account of this, the modern progress-directed world-view evidences a certain arrogance towards the past. Things are always better than they were and they'll just keep getting better and better. But if the future will be better than the past it follows that it will also be better than the present. The present is somehow transitory and less than sovereign in its own right as projects become entirely future-directed, but towards a future that never really arrives, that never *can* arrive. As Oscar Wilde remarked that fashion was "a form of ugliness so intolerable that we have to alter it every six months", so too the present contains a restlessness towards something better that is always underway. If old fashion is one domain where this is especially noticeable, so too are items of past technology, even of the recent past, which once excited admiration at their "cutting edge" quality, and now strike us as hopelessly antiquated.

---

[21] When the author was leaving school in 1980, the air was full of utopian talk about the near imminent liberation offered by the 'silicon chip.' We were offered a future in which we would work two or three days a week and spend the rest of our time pursuing edifying and self-enhancing interests. The reality has been quite the opposite as computerised systems, mobile telephony and the e mail have accelerated commerce making greater demands on employees and effectively breaking down the sharp barrier that once existed between work and leisure time. We are all instantly contactable and *expected* to be so.

The inception of liberalism and its meaning for the crisis

Turning to the political sphere, we find something complementary to the development of the modern scientific project. Classical liberalism presupposes the primacy of the individual and aims at maximising the conditions for the flourishing of private life even at the expense of the public sphere. According to classical liberalism, the public sphere is to be reorganised so as to facilitate the pursuit of purely private goals – hence the traditional hostility shown by liberalism towards the state, especially in the US, the purest instantiation of the liberal state in modernity. This is entirely in harmony with the hedonic aims of technological science, which I discuss below. In order to secure, maximise and sustain the new hedonic private bourgeois lifestyle, the domination of nature promised by the new science goes hand in hand with securing a social environment where privatisation is systematically privileged and in which the potential threat to this kind of social ideal posed by other human beings – the Hobbesian war of all against all - is contained as much as possible. The modern project requires the maximisation of civil peace and stability.

In *Leviathan* XIII Hobbes states that "the passions that incline men to peace are: fear of death; desire of such things as are necessary to commodious living; and a hope by their industry to obtain them." The (in)famous state of nature supposedly describes the constitution of each human being in their natural state as being intrinsically anti-social. This opens up a breach with the ancient and medieval principle that man is, in essence and therefore by nature, a social being.[22] Civil peace is a necessary condition for the cultivation of technical domination of nature and the development of commerce which is ultimately pursued for the sake of commodious living and, negatively, by the fear of violent death, which is for Hobbes the greatest evil.

---

[22] Aristotle describes the human as the *zoon politikon*, the political animal.

It is precisely considerations such as these which motivated the radically new political philosophy of Thomas Hobbes, which according to some commentators, marks the inception of the modern liberal polity as opposed to another view where it is customary to accord John Locke this distinction.[23] There is even a good case to be made for according this status to Spinoza, who certainly adumbrates a radical liberal politics prior to either Hobbes or Locke.

Francis Bacon had already realised, at the beginning of the 17th century, that the new scientific project was of such enormous magnitude as would require profound political and social changes. For present purposes I will merely assert that the 17th century inaugurates a socio-political revolution in the advanced states of Europe that culminates, in Britain, in the Glorious Revolution, and this same trend will eventually see a less peaceful accommodation in the streets of Paris in 1789.[24]

That Hobbes identifies the state of nature in the way that he does has immense consequences for the development of liberalism. This is rooted in his moral anthropology which sees man as evil, as having an ineluctable and indefeasible disposition to pursue self-interest on account of his corporeality.[25] On Hobbes's neo-Manichaean account

---

[23] Hobbes as father of liberalism is the view associated primarily with Leo Strauss: "If we may call liberalism that political doctrine which regards as the fundamental political fact the rights, as distinguished from the duties, of man and which identifies the function of the state with the protection or the safeguarding of those rights, we must say that the founder of liberalism was Hobbes." *NRH*, p 181.

[24] Unlike their English counterparts, they did not, for whatever reasons, make an accommodation with the new rising bourgeois class.

[25] The lineage of Hobbes' Voluntarism can be traced in a line of development back to Calvinist and Lutheran ideas of Unconditional Predestination (UP) which are in turn derived from an interpretation of St Augustine's theory of the will. The great historian of the early Church, Henry Chadwick sees a Gnostic origin for the doctrine of UP, *History of the Church* p 38. Augustine's views on the will show that he has not entirely broken free from his earlier Manichaeism.

we are dominated and ruled by our passions, *pace* Callicles and Thrasymachus, the advocates of a proto-Hobbesian views in Plato's *Gorgias* and *Republic* respectively. To Hobbes, the worst evil that can be suffered is a violent death although death itself is deemed an evil *simpliciter*.[26] The state for Hobbes exists to protect the lives of *individuals*, not of groupings, for example, the family or tribe. The state is there to shield the individual from what he conceives as the worst evil. This may also account for Hobbes' downgrading of the martial virtues – he denies, for example, that courage is a virtue and he says that a man who deserts in battle is not guilty of an injustice but only of something dishonourable.[27] Needless to say no army could ever exist if this were to be affirmed but nevertheless Hobbes has to take this position if he is going to be consistent with his commitment to an individualistic anthropology.

---

[26] *De Cive* ch I, section vii "Among so many dangers therefore, as the naturall lusts of men do daily threaten each other withall, to have a care of ones selfe is not a matter so scornfully to be lookt upon, as if so be there had not been a power and will left in one to have done otherwise; for every man is desirous of what is good for him, and shuns what is evill, but chiefly the chiefest of naturall evills, which is Death; and this he doth, by a certain impulsion of nature, no lesse than that whereby a Stone moves downward: It is therefore neither absurd, nor reprehensible; neither against the dictates of true reason for a man to use all his endeavours to preserve and defend his Body, and the Members thereof from death and sorrowes . . ." In the naturalistic terms that Hobbes adheres to, it follows that death would be the greatest evil. Contrast this with the attitude of Socrates: "For let me tell you, gentlemen, that to be afraid of death is only another form of thinking that one is wise when one is not; it is to think that one knows what one does not know. No one knows with regard to death whether it is not really the greatest blessing that can happen to a man, but people dread it as though they were certain that it was the greatest evil, and this ignorance, which thinks that it knows what it does not, must surely be ignorance most culpable." *Apology* 29a-b; see also *Phaedo* 62-69 for a general discussion of death and the philosopher's attitude to it, in striking contrast to the views of Hobbes about both death and philosophy.

[27] *Leviathan* xxi, 16.

In this we seem to have discovered a contradiction at the core of liberalism. How can the state be an instrument of protection for the individual's primary and immutable right to self-preservation, according to Hobbes, and yet, in the pursuance of this aim, demand the individual to put himself in harm's way? How then can it carry out its function if it cannot formulate a compelling argument as to why the citizen soldier may have to lay down his life for the state when it is threatened? This is just one example of the conflicted nature of classical liberalism but it is a glaring one as military defence touches on the primary function of the state.[28] There are others but it is enough for us to recognise this tension as a possible or even likely source of the legitimacy crisis and the problem of personal freedom diagnosed by John Dillon. The primacy of the individual and the aim of the state as protector of the individual sets up a profound and ineradicable discordance at the core of modern liberal politics: how can private selfishness be squared with public spiritedness? It seems that only through invoking arbitrary conditions that this discord can be evaded. The modern state sends out mixed messages – lauding selfishness whilst appealing to the common good – but this tension can only be *evaded* not resolved.

The ethical foundations of modernity

Thirdly we come on to the ethical dimension of modernity from which the problem of authority and the limits of freedom emerge in the political sphere. Let us return to Descartes for a moment. Unlike Hobbes, he still retains a link with the ancient conception of virtue in

---

[28] Another, which I cannot explore further here, would go something like this: how can a communal good arise from individual selfishness, or what C B Macpherson calls possessive individualism?

a more classical formulation of Epicureanism. Virtue he describes as resolutely willed constancy and is therefore the sovereign good, but happiness, as contentment, is also included in his conception of the good life such that he can go on to claim to have reconciled Zeno of Citium with Epicurus.[29] With Zeno he takes virtue to be the supreme good; with Epicurus he accepts the ultimate importance of contentment "to which he gave the name pleasure."

Descartes seemingly cannot decide whether or not the aim of life is cultivating virtue or achieving an inner tranquillity won through detachment (*ataraxia*). Perhaps *ataraxia* is achieved by cultivating virtue ("resolutely willed constancy"), but then we would need to discover precisely what he has in mind when he talks about virtue. Space restrictions prevent us from exploring this interesting puzzle any further – however we do need to see how he sets out, most explicitly, the neo-Epicurean ethical basis of modern techno-science which for Hobbes is taken up into the political.

It is in the Sixth *Discourse on the Method* that we find a very clear programmatic statement from Descartes concerning the instrumental and technological essence of the new science and its ethical foundation. It will be worth quoting this at length:

"But as soon as I had acquired some general notions respecting physics I began to test them in various particular problems, and observed how far they can carry us, and how much they differ from the principles that have been employed up to the present time. I believed that I could not keep them concealed without sinning grievously against the law by which we are bound to promote, as far as we can, the general good of mankind. For by these notions in physics I perceived it to be possible to arrive at

---

[29] Zeno of Citium is the founder of the Stoa as distinct from Zeno of Elea who set out to disprove plurality and motion through his famous paradoxes.

knowledge highly useful in life. In place of the speculative philosophy usually taught in the schools, it would be possible to discover a practical approach. By means of this, knowing the force and action of fire, water, air, the stars, the heavens, and all the other bodies that surround us—as distinctly as we know the various crafts of our artisans—we might also *apply* them in the same way to all the uses to which they are adapted, and thus render ourselves the lords and possessors of nature.

And this is a result to be desired, not only to promote invention of an infinity of arts—by which we might be enabled to enjoy without any trouble the fruits of the earth, and all its comforts—but also and especially for the preservation of health. This is, without doubt, of all the blessings of this life, the first and fundamental one. For the mind is so intimately dependent upon the condition and relation of the organs of the body, that if any means are ever to be found to render men wiser and more ingenious than hitherto, I believe that it is in medicine they must be sought for. It is true that the science of medicine, as it now exists, contains a few things whose utility is very remarkable. But without any wish to depreciate it, I am confident that there is no one—even among those whose profession it is—who does not admit that all at present known in it is almost nothing in comparison of what remains to be discovered; and that we could free ourselves from an infinity of maladies of body as well as of mind—and perhaps also even from the debility of age—if we had sufficiently ample knowledge of their causes, and of all the remedies provided for us by nature."[30]

[30] René Descartes *Discourse on the Method* (1637) VI.

Here we can see Descartes explicitly enunciating and commending an Epicurean ethical aim as the basis and motivation for the new science. It is simply assumed that the "general good of mankind" consists in enjoying the fruits of the earth, maintaining health and prolonging life for as long as possible. In order to bring this about we have to become the "lords and possessors of nature." Whilst Descartes still retains a traditional attitude towards the virtues, as opposed to Hobbes who does away with them altogether, a fundamental agreement emerges between these foundational modernists whereby ethical hedonism becomes politically programmatic and will henceforth guide the social and political revolution that is a necessary condition for its execution. The underlying tension will emerge more fully at a much later stage when the first major fruits of this project emerge in the form of consumerism in the early 20th century. I take consumerism to be the extension of possessive individualism and 'commodious living' to the masses. Prior to the early 20th century commodious living was the exclusive preserve of the aristocracy and the bourgeoisie.

Blumenberg's judgement that modernity reduces to the self-assertion of the will, Hobbes' anthropology of the dominion of the passions and the need for external constraint by the Leviathan state (as opposed to the Platonic call for the cultivation of the virtues and the rule of the wise), and the Baconian project of mastery of nature, in short; what I have been calling the materialist Neo-epicurean metaphysical and political dispensation inaugurated in the 17th century, *has run its course* as we face into the myriad crises that sprout Hydra-like in every domain we care to look at and that John Dillon diagnoses in part.

If anyone still doubts this, we need only refer to the sacred principle that is regularly intoned and of which its mere mention automatically trumps all other considerations, that is: growth. The principle of growth cannot acknowledge limit or what the Greeks called *peras*.

However, the world is finite and so are its so-called "resources". There is a mathematical formula that measures exponential growth, something we rarely, if ever, hear the acolytes of the cult of growth speaking about. A steady 7% growth per annum takes only 10 years for the thing growing to double in size. If oil consumption grows by between 3 and 4 percent per annum - we can expect this to increase as India and China modernise - this effectively means *production* will have to double within 20 years. Unfortunately oil reserves do not follow this growth and this factor alone seems to spell doom for a civilisation that is founded on a carbon fuels-based growth model. Growth of consumption and the natural limitation of most other resources sets up an alarming prospect for this century. But this sacred principle despite these inescapable barriers still governs everything even to the point where its measured presence is a source of great happiness, its absence, recession, is evil and the occasion for mandatory mass doom and gloom.

Close readers of Plato will not be surprised by all this. The modern project as I have described it is really nothing less than the historical expression of the view that Callicles represents in Plato's *Gorgias*. Callicles' position, (*Gorg* 494a – 95a) can be summarised as follows: pleasure is bound up in the process of satisfying wants like hunger and thirst and with their satisfaction the pleasure ceases, and since pleasure and good are identical – there are no bad pleasures – therefore, happiness lies in letting the appetites grow as big as possible and ensuring the means of feeding them.

Here is how he puts it:

> " . . . nature reveals that it's a just thing for the better man and the more capable man to have a greater share than the worse man and the less capable man. Nature shows that this is so in many places; both among the other animals and in whole cities and races of men, it shows that this is what justice has been decided to be: that the superior rule the inferior and have a

greater share than they. For what sort of justice did Xerxes go by when he campaigned against Greece, or his father when he campaigned against Scythia? Countless other such examples could be mentioned. I believe that these men do these things in accordance with the nature of what is just – yes, by Zeus, in accordance with the law of nature, and presumably not with the one we institute. (*Gorg* 483d-e)

Socrates opposes this viewpoint with great passion - we rarely see Socrates getting passionate - and when Callicles eventually refuses discourse, Socrates resorts to vehement exhortation even to the point of invoking the prospect of a kind of damnation for those who give themselves over to excess (*pleonexia*) and the overthrow of limits. What is interesting in this exchange is that both Callicles and Socrates agree implicitly that mankind ought to take its lead from nature and model itself upon it. Some students of Plato even suggest that the *Timaeus* was motivated by the ethical imperative to demonstrate the orderliness of nature, a perspective that would go a considerable way in explaining the significance of the battle with the Atlanteans at the beginning (*Tim* 20d–26d) who embody a great many of the very traits that Callicles praises. Socrates' and Callicles' disagreement reduces to the question – what is nature? Callicles thinks it natural to give the appetites free reign, whereas Socrates sees nature as the tangible manifestation of a divine order.

"Yes, Callicles, wise men claim that the community (*koinonia*) and friendship (*philia*), orderliness (*kosmiotes*), self-control (*sophrosune*), and justice (*dikaiotes*) hold together heaven and earth, and gods and men, and that is why they call this universe a world order (*kosmos*), my friend, and not a disorder (*akosmia*) or lack of control (*akolasia*). I believe that you don't pay attention to these facts even though you are a wise man in these matters. You've failed to notice that proportionate equality (*he isotes he geometrike*) has great power among both gods and men, and you suppose that you ought to practise getting the greater share (*pleonexia*). That's because you neglect geometry." (*Gorg* 508a, tr Zeyl)

It must surely be clear to us now, given the very grave problems afflicting western civilisation, that the kind of principles upon which the world was re-founded in the 17th century - and which had already been critically anticipated in Platonic dialogues like the *Gorgias* - and which reach full expression in the pleonectic consumerist model, is coming to an end. Something else will surely arise from the remnants of an untenable and discredited way of being and doing – what that will be is surely impossible for us to specify in any detail. However, it is clear that sustainability, acknowledgement of limits, a rediscovery of the cardinal virtues and wisdom above all, the primacy of the common good in human affairs, and, of course, a recovery of man's divine part and destiny, will, one feels, be rediscovered, by dint of external necessity if nothing else, and as indispensable components of a decent and realistic human existence. It is in this sense that Platonism, not as a set of specific doctrines nor as a historical body of thought but as a fundamental conception of reality, retains the same urgency now as it did when Plato set about writing the dialogues. Platonism in essence is one of the two fundamental conceptions of reality that suggest themselves when the human mind turns to consider the nature of reality. The other is materialism or metaphysical naturalism which we have cursorily reviewed. If there is a growing perception that metaphysical naturalism has failed to meet the deep human need for integration with the whole of reality – and this I understand to be the basic meaning of *eudaimonia* – then the coming swing will be in some kind of broadly Platonic direction, albeit in specific ways that are hardly imaginable to us now.

The Dublin Centre
for the Study of the Platonic Tradition
www.tcd.ie/Classics/cspt

In 2006, The Dublin Centre for the Study of the Platonic Tradition inaugurated an ongoing series of public lectures on the general theme of `Platonism and the World Crisis' (see Introduction). The purpose here was to invite eminent figures from Irish intellectual and cultural life to deliver a public lecture on a topic that comes under the aegis of the series theme. These lectures are now being published in pamphlet form as a permanent record of these evenings. This series was conceived to become the public face of the Centre, the visible aspect of our existence, so to speak; but what of the Centre itself as a scholarly institution, its main *raison d'etre?* Who are we and what do we do?

General Introduction

The Centre, founded in 1997, is designed to coordinate and direct activities in the area of the history of Platonism (including Christian, Jewish and Islamic Platonism) in the Greater Dublin area, bringing together scholars working at Trinity College, Dublin, the National University of Ireland-Dublin, and the National University of Ireland-Maynooth, together with All Hallows College, Drumcondra.

Its activities include:
- the organising of seminars, colloquia and lectures by visiting scholars
- the supervision of graduate students
- the publication of texts and monographs.

In cooperation with the various constituent departments, the Centre offers degrees in Platonic Studies from Master's through to Doctoral levels.

The Centre Library and Reading Room

On October 21, 2004, there took place the formal opening by the Provost, Prof John Hegarty, of the Library and Reading Room of the Centre. This is the culmination of some years of planning, and resulted from the acceptance by Trinity College of the offer by the Director, Professor John Dillon to offer his library of books of Greek philosophy to the College on condition that premises would be made available to house it. Space was found in the lower level of the 1937 Reading Room in Front Square, and so the Centre now at last has a physical base, and a useful research tool in the form of a collection of about 2500 books on the history of Platonism, together with all of the basic primary texts. This marks the Centre collection as the largest concentration of materials relating to Platonism in the country. Students also have. of course, access to the holdings of the Main Library, which are considerable.

The Stephen MacKenna Lecture Series

Apart from the present series, the Centre hosts a more academic lecture series, named in honour of the great Irish translator of Plotinus, Stephen MacKenna, designed to honour a succession of the most distinguished scholars in the area of Neoplatonism. As of 2010, this has passed into its tenth year, having on May 19 hosted Prof Christopher Gill. Previous MacKenna lecturers include Prof Werner Beierwaltes (1999), Prof John M Rist (2001), Prof Carlos Steel of the University of Leuven (2002), Prof Dominic O'Meara (2005), Professor Eyjolfur Emilsson of Oslo (2006), and Prof Christopher Rowe (2009).

The International Plato Society

The Centre had the honour of holding the Presidency of the International Plato Society, a position that is held for three years, culminating in a major conference, which was held in Trinity College in July 2007.

The Prometheus Trust Catalogue

Platonic Texts and Translations Series

I Iamblichi Chalcidensis in Platonis Dialogos Commentariorum Fragmenta   John M Dillon   978-1-898910 45 9

II The Greek Commentaries on Plato's Phaedo (I – Olympiodorus)

L G Westerink   978-1-898910-46-6

III The Greek Commentaries on Plato's Phaedo (II – Damascius)

L G Westerink   978-1-898910-47-3

IV Damascius, Lectures on the Philebus

L G Westerink   978-1-898910-48-0

V The Anonymous Prolegomena to Platonic Philosophy

L G Westerink   In preparation

VI Proclus' Commentary on the First Alcibiades

Text: L G Westerink. Translation: W O'Neill.   In preparation

The Thomas Taylor Series

1 Proclus' Elements of Theology

Proclus' Elements of Theology - 211 propositions which frame the metaphysics of the Late Athenian Academy. 978-1-898910-00-8

2 Select Works of Porphyry

Abstinence from Animal Food; Auxiliaries to the Perception of Intelligibles; Concerning Homer's Cave of the Nymphs; Taylor on the Wanderings of Ulysses. 978-1-898910-01-5

3 Collected Writings of Plotinus

Twenty-seven treatises being all the writings of Plotinus translated by Taylor. 978-1-898910-02-2

4 Writings on the Gods & the World

Sallust On the Gods & the World; Sentences of Demophilus; Ocellus on the Nature of the Universe; Taurus and Proclus on the Eternity of the World; Maternus on the Thema Mundi; The Emperor Julian's Orations to the Mother of Gods and to the Sovereign Sun; Synesius on Providence; Taylor's essays on the Mythology and the Theology of the Greeks. 978-1-898910-03-9

5 Hymns and Initiations

The Hymns of Orpheus together with all the published hymns translated or written by Taylor; Taylor's 1824 essay on Orpheus (together with the 1787 version). 978-1-898910-04-6

6 Dissertations of Maximus Tyrius

Forty-one treatises from the middle Platonist, and an essay from Taylor, The Triumph of the Wise Man over Fortune. 978-1-898910-05-3

7 Oracles and Mysteries

A Collection of Chaldean Oracles; Essays on the Eleusinian and Bacchic Mysteries; The History of the Restoration of the Platonic Theology; On the Immortality of the Soul. 978-1-898910-06-0

8 The Theology of Plato

The six books of Proclus on the Theology of Plato; to which is added a further book (by Taylor), replacing the original seventh book by Proclus, now lost. Extensive introduction and notes are also added. 978-1-898910-07-7

9 Works of Plato I

Taylor's General Introduction, Life of Plato, First Alcibiades (with much of Proclus' Commentary), Republic (with a section of Proclus' Commentary). 978-1-898910-08-4

10 Works of Plato II

Laws, Epinomis, Timæus (with notes from Proclus' Commentary), Critias. 978-1-898910-09-1

11 Works of Plato III

Parmenides (with a large part of Proclus' Commentary), Sophista, Phædrus (with notes from Hermias' Commentary), Greater Hippias, Banquet. 978-1-898910-10-7

12 Works of Plato IV

Theætetus, Politicus, Minos, Apology of Socrates, Crito, Phædo (with notes from the Commentaries of Damascius and Olympiodorus), Gorgias (with notes from the Commentary of Olympiodorus), Philebus (with notes from the Commentary of Olympiodorus), Second Alcibiades. 978-1-898910-11-4

13 Works of Plato V

Euthyphro, Meno, Protagoras, Theages, Laches, Lysis, Charmides, Lesser Hippias, Euthydemus, Hipparchus, Rivals, Menexenus, Clitopho, Io, Cratylus (together with virtually the whole of Proclus' Scholia), Epistles. An index to the extensive notes Taylor added to the 5 volumes. 978-1-898910-12-1

14 Apuleius' Golden Ass & Other Philosophical Writings

The Golden Ass (or Metamorphosis); On the Dæmon of Socrates; On the Philosophy of Plato. 978-1-898910-13-8

15 & 16 Proclus' Commentary on the Timæus of Plato

The Five Books of this Commentary in two volumes, with additional notes and short index. 978-1-898910-14-5 and 978-1-898910-15-2

17 Iamblichus on the Mysteries and Life of Pythagoras

Iamblichus On the Mysteries of the Egyptians, Chaldeans & Assyrians; Iamblichus' Life of Pythagoras; Fragments of the Ethical Writings of Pythagoreans; Political Fragments of Archytas, Charondas and other Pythagoreans. 978-1-898910-16-9

26 The Works of Aristotle VIII

History of Animals, & the Treatise on Physiognomy. 978-1-898910-25-1

27 The Works of Aristotle IX

The Parts of Animals; The Progressive Motions of Animals, The Problems; On Indivisible Lines. 978-1-898910-26-8

28 The Philosophy of Aristotle

Taylor's four part dissertation on the philosophy of Aristotle which outlines his primary teachings, the harmony of Plato and Aristotle, and modern misunderstandings of Aristotle. 978-1-898910-27-5

29 Proclus' Commentary on Euclid

Proclus' Commentary on the First Book of Euclid's Elements; Taylor's four part Dissertation on the Platonic Doctrine of Ideas, on Demonstrative Syllogism, On the Nature of the Soul, and on the True End of Geometry. 978-1-898910-28-2

30 The Theoretical Arithmetic of the Pythagoreans

The Theoretic Arithmetic of the Pythagoreans, Medicina Mentis, Nullities & Diverging Series, The Elements of a New Arithmetic Notation, Elements of True Arithmetic of Infinities. 978-1-898910-29-9

31 & 32 Pausanias' Guide to Greece

Pausanias' Guide to Greece (in two volumes) with illustrations and extensive notes on mythology. 978-1-898910-30-5 & 978-1-898910-31-2

33 Against the Christians and Other Writings

The Arguments of Julian Against the Christians; Celsus, Porphyry and Julian Against the Christians; Writings of Thomas Taylor from his Collectanea, his Miscellanies in Prose and Verse, and his short works On Critics, An Answer to Dr Gillies, A Vindication of the Rights of Brutes, and his articles from the Classical Journal. Included is a Thomas Taylor bibliography. 978-1-898910-32-9

Other titles available from the Prometheus Trust

Philosophy as a Rite of Rebirth – From Ancient Egypt to Neoplatonism   Algis Uždavinys   978-1-898910-35-0

The Philosophy of Proclus – the Final Phase of Ancient Thought
L J Rosán   978 1 898910 44 2

The Seven Myths of the Soul   Tim Addey   978-1-898910-37-4

An Index to Plato - A Subject Index using Stephanus pagination
978-1-898910-34-3

Students' Edition Paperbacks

The Symposium of Plato
Trans. Floyer Sydenham & Thomas Taylor. Includes Plotinus' On Love (En III, 5), and introductory essays.   978-1-898910-38-1

Know Thyself – The First Alcibiades & Commentary
Trans. Floyer Sydenham & Thomas Taylor. With introductory essays.
978-1-898910-39-8

Beyond the Shadows - The Metaphysics of the Platonic Tradition
Guy Wyndham-Jones and Tim Addey   978-1-898910-40-4

The Unfolding Wings - The Way of Perfection in the Platonic Tradition   Tim Addey   978-1-898910-41-1

The Prometheus Trust is a registered UK charity. Apart from its publishing activities, it also offers education in philosophy, public lectures, workshops and conferences. For further details please visit the Prometheus Trust website at: www.prometheustrust.co.uk